LIVE AND BE FREE THRU PSYCHO-CYBERNETICS

**Co-Authored by
Maxwell Maltz, M.D.**

and

Charles Schreiber, F.A.R.A

www.snowballpublishing.com

info@snowballpublishing.com

For information regarding special discounts for bulk purchases, please contact
Snowball Publishing at

sales@snowballpublishing.com

Contents

Preface

I have written more than eight books on Psycho-Cybernetics which have been read by tens of millions of persons throughout the world. Co-authoring a book on a subject I have been very deeply involved in is a very important undertaking; therefore, it is with a great deal of enthusiasm and respect that I welcome the opportunity to introduce my co-author, Mr. Charles Schreiber.

In my years of traveling, lecturing, and writing, I have found one man unequaled in his ability to influence life around him through Psycho-Cybernetics. The uniqueness of Charles Schreiber is not just in the personal and business success *he* has achieved, but in his talent for TEACHING others how to gain more from *their* lives through Psycho-Cybernetics.

I became aware of his abilities in 1965, and for the past five years he has been my personal ambassador, conducting seminars, workshops and evening classes to businesses, individuals and families. In 1973 Charles Schreiber was appointed National Director of Workshops and Seminars. His files are filled with letters of appreciation and endorsement from his students.

What you are about to read will be the first book I have co-authored on Psycho-Cybernetics. It offers you a "self-study" program under the guiding hand of Charles Schreiber. The book provides you with practical tools; new, easy-to-grasp techniques for achieving greater personal growth. You will learn to form the habit of thinking positively, and it will reflect itself in your daily life. Now we have made available through this book, a program for you to follow, to learn how to improve your life in the privacy of your home or business.

I predict the start of a new life for you—living free—in just twenty-one days. I know this book will deepen your knowledge, and show you how to be "goal-directed." You will live a more successful, happy life, because you will have learned to LIVE and FEEL FREE!

Maxwell Maltz, M.D., F.I.C.S.

1

The Chief Purpose
of This Book

The intention of this book is to assist you in becoming a tremendously more *effective* person, not just in one area, but in every phase of your life. The knowledge gained from this book will help expand your thinking to understand yourself. It differs from many books of this nature in that it deals with an emphasis on practical, usable tools.

Accept in Two Basic Ways

As you progress from step to step in your understanding of the principles involved, undoubtedly you will accept them in one of two basic ways:

You may regard them as an interesting mental exercise whereby you may gain knowledge of practical psychology worthy of careful evaluation. In the event that this is your attitude, you will achieve a greater understanding of how and why people act and react as they do, and will vaguely sense that if you *wanted* to do something about becoming a more effective person, you could do so.

On the other hand, you may test the tools and ideas

given and find it is not necessary to *believe*—the mere knowledge that you *tried* them and they *did* work is enough. You will find that all these techniques work if you will let them. If you acquire this state of mind you will surely be entering one of the most exciting periods of your life, and the learning and growing process started will extend far beyond the reading of this book and literally change the rest of your life.

Confirmed by Our Own Experience

Perhaps the best introduction to the philosophy we wish to advocate would be to tell you that we believe a person is not born happy—he *learns* to be happy.

We make only one claim for the formulas and ideas offered; they are confirmed by our own observation and experience, and they have increased our own happiness and peace of mind whenever we have acted in accord with them.

Many of the ideas and techniques we will review are as old as recorded history—thoroughly tested and proven. Some will be familiar to you, some even may seem over-simplified.

Contents Show You How

We are all attempting to get more living out of life, make more of ourselves, *learn* more, *do* more, *be* more than we are.

This book will show you *How To:*

Reach more of your goals
Use more of your potential
Develop attitudes that will get you what you want
Become a more successful person

You Can Only Prove By Doing

The only way to demonstrate the ideas presented in this book is to translate them into action; put them to the test and then decide how effective they are. No amount of debate or discussion can give you proof that these theories work, but if you will actually follow them for twenty-one days, you will be able to judge the outcome for yourself.*

Promise

We promise you if you will make use of the simple ideas and formulas contained in this book, the results will be tangible, they will be measureable, and they will be soon. The time investment you make in the program is not just an investment in a success program; it is an investment in your future, your success and your happiness.

Basic Factors for Success

Many books have been written about the secrets of success, as though there are dark, mysterious truths that lie back of it. There are no hidden secrets or mysterious truths; the reasons for success are plain and simple—you can learn and can master them.

Why People Don't Succeed

There are countless individuals who seem to have all the needed requirements for success, yet they do not succeed. They have natural ability, education, attractive personalities, outstanding talents, yet they fail to make good. Why?

On the other hand, there are individuals who lack all these advantages. Yet they make outstanding successes in business and in their family and social life.

*For a person to experience a noticeable change in a mental picture, a minimum of twenty-one consecutive days must elapse.

People, with rare exceptions, do not fail because they lack knowledge, education or talents. They fail chiefly because of what they do not do.

One of the big reasons that most people go through life getting so little out of it is that *they do not really know what they want.* Things happen to them more by chance than by choice.

When a person stops seeking idle pleasure and begins *truly seeking success and happiness,* that is the *turning point* in his life. There is such a turning point in the life of every successful person. Therefore, the first step toward your success is for you to cause this turning point. *You and you alone, can do it.*

If this turning point has already come with you, and you are moving toward greater success and happiness, this will strengthen your determination and show you how to mobilize your ambitions and skills for a rich and happy life of accomplishment and fulfillment.

Determining Factors for Success

Do you know in what way the mind and a parachute are alike? They both must be open to function properly.

Psychologists have determined that only 15 percent of our knowledge is in technical training, and the balance of 85 percent is represented in *personal qualities,* such as the following:

Goal Oriented	Relaxation
Memory (re-call)	Personal Confidence
Creative	Friendlier
React Calmly	Decisive
Enthusiastic	Aggressive
Diplomatic	Getting Along with Others

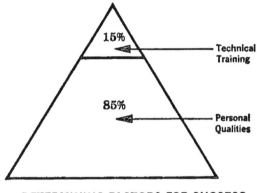

DETERMINING FACTORS FOR SUCCESS

The Conquest of Inner Space

Why can we move at such breathtaking speed to conquer the vast wonders of outer space, yet make virtually no progress at lighting up dark inner recesses of the human mind?

The giant rocket that carries our astronauts on their magic journey to the moon and the tiny cameras that let us more or less journey with them—these are testaments to man's rationality, his mastery of logic. But the stories told by the crewmen of the U.S.S. *Pueblo,* that speak of the hatreds and uncontrolled emotions that go back to Cain and Abel, have dogged mankind down through the course of human history.

Of course a reporter need not speculate on Vietnam or North Korea to see this darker side of man's nature. For the year of *Apollo 8* was also the year of the murders of Senator Robert Kennedy and Dr. Martin Luther King and many other violent indications that man is not nearly so smart as his technology would suggest.

Enjoyment of the magnificent technological feats involved in space travel is diminished by the certain knowl-

13

edge that probably more people are at work trying to figure out military applications than are busy trying to determine in what ways these achievements can be turned into the uplift of the whole human family.

We marvel at the ease with which man unlocked the secrets of the universe. *Why cannot they also uncover some of the dark mysteries within themselves?*—the things that make us the frail and destructive creatures that we are.

We may actually go down in history as the age that got a man on the moon before we had figured out a way to get the pigeons off the statues.

Avoid Debating

The ideas discussed are as old as recorded history and confirmed by all those who have tried them. The most important thing in studying the information in the book, right from the start, is to avoid debating about who is right and who is not.

A debate always follows discussions where one person deals in generalities and the other counters with specifics. The use of false analogies and syllogistic logic fuel the fire.

Why is it that another person sees things we do not see, or he fails to see things we see? Seeing things as they are is not as simple as it always supposed. The ability to deceive ourselves is boundless. We build our own illusions of reality.

> **What you see (in your imagination) is what you get.**
> **What you think (about) is what you get.**
> **You receive the net results of what you think (about.)**

It is silly to think that those who make no effort and are undisciplined could possibly know what these things are and, presuming that the other person knows, it is obviously absurd to enter into a debate with this false assumption as a premise.

14

Another false assumption that infiltrates through a debate is that the other person can change his basic values suddenly. This is not true and the reason it is not true is that at any given moment we have become who we are because of our past (conditioning). We remain as we are or change due to more or other conditioning. To suppose that something so laboriously built up can be altered suddenly by rational (intellectual) argument is remote.

Changing people's values and understanding, or whatever, occurs only when the change or idea was in work for some time before it surfaced publicly. It is ridiculous to assume you can produce changes in people suddenly, and only by means of argumentation. To change someone's mind is the result, not the cause, of changing him, since argumentation occurs from the kind of person he is already, not the other way around. Since arguments result from the kind of person one already is, it is easy to see why it is wrong to think you can argue someone into being another way.

We expect that if an idea or technique does not agree with your present thinking, you will not attempt to debate it, but to learn its validity by trying it in your life.

It is an unassailable fact that all of us possess infinitely more talent than we use. Therefore, it is logical to conclude that the measure of success we achieve is not dependent on how much we possess, but *how much we utilize*.

We Can Always Be Better

It is impossible for an individual to communicate to others all the knowledge of his real self. No one can ever exercise the full potential effectiveness of his real self. Every one of us has much room for improvement. Our real self is constantly moving toward, but never reaching, its ultimate goal. The real self is not passive, but is forever in motion; it is never really perfected and is perpetually in a developmental state.

Consequently, no one should merely aim to be a success, but should strive to be successful.

15

Discovery for Success

We will draw a triangle representing one person's potential and a second triangle representing another person's potential. The first person has a great amount of natural ability, outstanding talents, a broad education and an attractive personality. The second person does not have all of these advantages and has a much smaller potential. Which of these two persons would we say would be more successful?

Obviously we would all agree that it would be number one. But when this doesn't happen, how is it explained? The number two person far exceeds the number one in the degree of success accomplished. Most people are at a loss to explain this. What happened to number two to allow him to do this? The explanation is simple. He simply *used* a lot more of what he had and thereby attained a greater degree of success. To reiterate, if we draw a line across the following illustration in the lower part of triangle two and extended into triangle one, indicating the amount of potential used, it then becomes apparent why person number two will become more successful than number one.

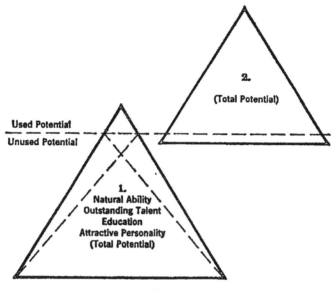

Used Potential

Unused Potential

2.
(Total Potential)

1.
Natural Ability
Outstanding Talent
Education
Attractive Personality
(Total Potential)

REQUIREMENTS FOR SUCCESS

The training, exercises and techniques you will use will enable you to bring out your unused potential, and be eminently more successful than you ever dreamed you could.

17

2

Two Images

You have within you a deep desire to perform something or to be someone which will bring real happiness, satisfaction and peace of mind into your life. While you usually consider this desire to be no more than wishful thinking, being impossible to attain, you never forget it.

The fact that you have this desire is evidence that it is attainable. You hold two pictures of yourself in your mind. The first is a picture of the person you know yourself to be—a person with whom in many ways you are dissatisfied. The second is a picture of the person you'd like to be—a relaxed, enthusiastic, confident, decisive person ready to meet any situation and master it, respected by all those who know you.

The contrast between the person you are and this inner vision of what you might be is the *Divine Discontent* in you; it accounts for all your growth and progress. It is not a device by which nature tantalizes you. It is not contained within you as a seed of frustration and unhappiness.

It is the creative urge within you which builds the desire to grow. Nature has equated this urge within you with a built-in equipment that enables you to grow and to continue growing mentally and spiritually as long as you live.

You want to feel secure, to be loved, to be important, appreciated, needed and to be respected. You are not unique in these feelings. All human beings have them.

This book will outline a program for you and show you how to put this built-in equipment to work, and how to handle it in such a way that you may become the person tomorrow that you envision today.

3

Acquiring Knowledge

*Acquiring Knowledge is Passive—
Experience Is Active*

People gain knowledge through the reading of books, but to really *experience* one must react psychologically and imaginatively to that knowledge.

Experience Necessary

If you follow the ideas set forth here, you will actually be forced to *experience*. Merely talking about them will not verify their worth in your life. The only way you can prove they are valid is to try them out and then decide for yourself what effect they have upon you as an individual. Put them into action, reserving your judgment until you have given them an opportunity to work for you.

What is the magic of carrying out these rules, regulations and suggestions? Just this—a deep driving desire to learn and a vigorous determination to start today and never stop. The only way we can develop such an urge is to constantly remind ourselves of how important these principles are to us.

There is no Other Way

Say to yourself over and over and over: *My peace of mind, my happiness, my health and even my income will, in the long run, depend largely on applying the old, obvious and eternal truths that have been described.* Write this material down, keep this knowledge near you, glance at it often.

Remember that the use of these principles can be made habitual and unconscious only by a *constant* and *vigorous* campaign of review and application. *There is no other way.*

When you acquire knowledge only intellectually, you will never *learn*. You can *learn* only by doing. If you want to master these principles, study them thoroughly. Do something about them in *applying* them at every opportunity. If you don't, you will forget them.

Until knowledge is activated into a useful advantage, it is worthless.

Only knowledge that is used flows to the conscious mind. You will probably find it difficult to apply this all the time. You are not merely trying to acquire information, you are attempting to *form a new habit pattern.* This will require time, persistence and daily application. Use these principles and they will achieve magic for you.

Know Thyself

From Socrates, the first great teacher of success, down to the present day, wise men have said, "Know thyself." This is essential for you. You are unique. There is not now, nor will there ever be, another human being exactly like you. However, it is true that you have the same basic desires that every other human being has. What makes the difference is the degree of intensity of these desires. This defines what is important to you, and what you think is important determines what you do.

21

Basic Desires

Human beings are all moved by four basic desires; they are, at the same time, man's four basic goals:

Security (physical-emotional-financial)
Love
Ego Satisfaction
Bodily Comforts and Possessions

The difference of the level of these four desires is what distinguishes one person from another. What makes you an individual is the strength and degree of your desire to meet these basic goals.

Objectives

Objectives are defined duties and responsibilities. They set the pattern of your behavior. You cause a "turning point" in your life when you recognize your duties and responsibilities to *yourself, your loved ones,* and to *the company* which provides your livelihood and then accept these duties and responsibilities and proceed to carry them out to the full extent of your ability.

We repeat for emphasis: The "turning point" in your life will come when you recognize your duties and responsibilities to yourself, your loved ones and your company; when you accept these duties and responsibilities and proceed to carry them out to the full extent of your ability.

You will carry out your duties and responsibilities when you define your goals, lay out a plan for reaching them, establish controls, and generate within yourself the power of self-motivation.

Value of Setting Goals

The value to you in setting definite objectives or goals is that you link your thinking to a purpose. You no longer daydream. You know where you are going, and your thoughts and actions are concentrated on getting you there.

Your personal improvement is the greatest consideration in your life. Yes, without question or a doubt, your personal development is the most important thing in your life.

Change Necessary

As you follow these suggestions, you will begin to improve immediately. You will note a decided change in your thinking, in your power of understanding, in your ability to solve your problems and to express your thoughts forcefully, fluently, and convincingly.

Does this sound as though we are offering you the world in a neat package? We are. It is not a wild promise and will surely be fulfilled. We have seen remarkable changes in the lives of men and women who have made the sincere effort and followed these simple procedures.

A Great Discovery

But, first, each and every one of them changed their attitudes of mind. In the year 1900, William James, Professor at Harvard, Medical Doctor, Psychiatrist, Philosopher, and one of the foremost thinkers this nation has produced, made a profound statement.

Nineteen hundred—this was the year when the electric light and the automobile came into being. He did not mention them. "The greatest discovery of my generation," he said, "is that human beings may alter their lives by altering their attitudes of mind."

Everything in your life depends on your mental attitude,

and the important thing to remember is that *you control your mental attitude.* In fact, it is the one thing in your life that you can *absolutely control.*

Desire to Succeed

Once you decide that you are going to make your hopes and dreams realities, turn wishes into facts and desires into solid achievements, you are taking the first step on the path to success. You have generated within yourself the desire to succeed. Daily, as you work with this program, your confidence will grow and hasten your progress toward your goal. Your mental attitude will undergo great change. You will believe you can. And when you believe you can—*YOU CAN!*

Nature has given every human being at birth a built-in automatic success mechanism. Human beings are gifted with creative imagination and can formulate their own goals. For our own peace of mind and happiness, it is imperative that we do this. The ideas in this book are designed specifically to help you achieve the goals that you set for yourself. It deals exclusively with the one most important factor to you—*your own personal goals.*

You Must Do It

You must realize that you are the only one who can make it effective. This program will tell you what to do and how to do it. But *you must do it,* consciously following the directions on how to get to where you want to go.

Become Emotionally Involved

Reading this book will not make you a success. You must become emotionally involved and tailor the principles enumerated to fill the needs and requirements for your own progress. Therefore, do not rush through this book. Take as much time as needed and work out the pattern for your success with careful thought. The more sound thinking you do at this time about your future progress, the better will be your plan and the greater your success.

Generate Enthusiasm

Many books and talks by the thousands tell you that you must be self-motivated; that you must be enthusiastic; that enthusiasm overcomes all obstacles; that nothing great is possible without enthusiasm; that the enthusiastic individual, while often dissatisfied, is never discouraged or negative. This is all true, but these books and talks do not tell in plain, understandable language *how you can generate this enthusiasm* and become self-motivated.

Yet, the way is simple. You must be motivated toward something. You must be enthused about something. That is why you were told to *set a goal* for yourself—one that you can reach.

Then you must use the most powerful force in all history of man's achievement, IMAGINATION.

4

The Strangest Secret

Even though this knowledge, as we have said, is as old as recorded history—the early wise men discovered it, and it appears again and again throughout the Bible—it remains a secret. This is strange, because most people who know about it do not understand it. Therefore, it remains the *strangest secret*. But you can dare to be different. Then you will be different from the millions of unhappy people in this world. *You will know the truth that will set you free.*

Secret of Success

If you were aboLe to stop people on the street and ask them, "What is the secret of success?" maybe one out of fifty could tell you. Of all people, 95 percent are actually searching for the right to fail.

Suppose we were to tell a man that there is a mansion ready and waiting for his occupancy just over the hill. He wants to believe you, but he is unable to. He has been

26

fooled too many times by too many people, and he is not willing to risk being hurt again.

But the mansion actually exists whether he moves toward it or not. Whether he claims it or not, it is always there ready for him. This is our problem: the man will not walk toward the mansion until he sees it, and he cannot see it until he walks toward it.

This seems to be the dilemma we are all undertaking, and it is our job to get you to move forward far enough to catch your first glimpse of the mansion. Maybe you'll see only a small portion of it, but that is enough. You will have seen something that will make you curious, excited and eager.

The real secret is *goals;* people succeed with them and fail without them.

Something to Think About

Grant me the serenity to accept the things I cannot change, the courage to change the things I can, and the wisdom to know the difference.

5

Expectation of Change

How Soon Can You Expect Change?

How long will it be before you can actually use or experience these principles and notice a change?

Changes take place immediately, the very moment you read or learn in any way some fundamental principle for a more superior life. You then will experience some reaction. This reaction may be somewhat clouded, but if you are persistent, a more distinct understanding will emerge. A typical response is, "I'm not sure what is happening, but something different is occurring."

The constructive positive changes you make inside you will have a beneficial effect on your personality and all your activities.

Confusion is Helpful

As you think about what you are reading, do not be concerned about being confused. *Confusion is a genuine emotion.* A man has begun to understand himself when he can say, "I don't know," without being afraid. To realize you don't know is the beginning of knowing.

If an idea seems to be outside your comprehension, do not disregard it. There is no idea or principle that is incomprehensible to man. No matter how obscure, it exists in every human being.

As you progress toward change, a strange thing happens. Your confusion will grow just before you realize the truth for the first time (darkness before the dawn). A simple explanation is that you have become more aware of your confusion. You've brought it up to the conscious level, and you now discover that you didn't comprehend as much as you thought; this gives you a genuine understanding. The reason you fail to be really happy and to attain personal freedom is because you actually are unaware that such a state is attainable.

Need to be Aware of its Existence

In order for us to be motivated toward something, we must at least have a suspicion of its existence.

We are not discussing anything far-out or of no practical value. We are offering you a far better way to live that you can benefit from today. Finding it is only possible through an awareness that it does exist. What is really strange—we already know, but we are not aware that we know.

It is not necessary that you understand the basic mechanical principles of an automobile in order to drive it or ride in it. Therefore, you do not need totally to grasp the numerous changes that will take place within you. Let them happen. Relax with your studies of Psycho-Cybernetics. Read with a sense of exploration, seeing everything as good news, and enjoy the adventure.

29

6

As A Man Thinks

As A Man Thinks So He Is

As a man thinks, so he is; and as he continues to think, so he shall remain. This thought not only embraces man's being, but is so comprehensive as to reach out to all circumstances of his life. A man is what he thinks. His complete character is the sum of his thoughts and as long as he maintains those thoughts, he remains the same.

SOME MAY REACH FOR THE STARS,
OTHERS WILL END BEHIND BARS,
YET, WE WOULD ALL LIKE THE RIGHT,
TO FIND THE KEY TO SUCCESS,
THAT ELUSIVE RAY OF LIGHT,
THAT WILL LEAD TO HAPPINESS.

What do you think is holding this man behind the bars?
Obviously there are many ways he can get out. All of us are sometimes captured by some idea or situation, and put ourselves behind bars. We feel locked in. What could he possibly be saying to himself that is holding him there?

He could be saying:

"I don't want to get out."

"I don't see a way out," or simply

"I can't get out."

If he thinks and believes he can't get out—he can't.

As a man thinks, he is.

Psycho-Cybernetics Defined

Psycho-Cybernetics is defined as a method of steering yourself. Where do you want to steer yourself? If you don't know, you're in trouble. You are somewhat like the man who stands at the airline ticket counter and when asked, "Where do you want to go?" replies, "I don't

31

know," or says, "Give me a ticket to anywhere you choose." Does it make sense not to know, or to let somebody else choose your goal for you?

Psycho-Cybernetics is positive doing. It is a guide, a gateway to creative living. It is a way of life. *Psycho* means mind and *Cybernetics* is taken from a Greek word meaning "helmsman", a man who steers a ship to port.

This word has been coined to mean "steering your mind to a productive, useful, worthwhile, predetermined goal," so that you can reach the greatest port in the world, *peace of mind.*

From the beginning of recorded time, man has held, in one form or another, the concept that there is something guiding him, a guiding force outside himself. This belief has taken thousands of forms, but has persisted from primitive superstitions to the philosophy of our modern cultured societies.

Essence of Psycho-Cybernetics

The essence of Psycho-Cybernetics is that *our basic ultimate goals have already been predetermined.*

Man is teleological. He is motivated toward some ultimate goal having an ultimate meaning. Man in his existence on this earth does not know what this is. But when he is not moving in this direction, he gets negative feedback (Divine Discontent). We all came from someplace and we're going someplace. The architect of the universe did not build a stairway going nowhere. Man, by his very nature, is acting freely and normally when he is pursuing a precise objective and is working actively toward it. The feeling of contentment is a by-product of his goal, because when a person is working toward a definite goal, he is usually happy, no matter what his situation may be.

Only when man moves for accomplishment in life does he begin to fulfill the purpose inherent in the existence of life. Life calls for activity, and for man this activity needs to be purposeful in order to bring realization that it is meaningful.

Man's big goal is toward creative accomplishment.

32

Man Similar to a Machine

You are guided by your mind. Have you ever seen a tractor, a giant earth-moving machine—a tremendous, incredible machine, with a man sitting way up on top with a wheel in his hand guiding it. It occurred to us that there was a similarity between the human mind and this machine. Suppose you are at the controls of such a vast source of energy. Will you settle back and fold your arms and allow it to run itself into a ditch, or are you going to hold both hands on the wheel and control and direct the power to a specific, worthwhile goal. It's up to you.

Let's say we had two ocean-going liners—again, enormous machines. One, we staff with a full crew and give it a goal. It surely will get where it starts out to go 9,999 out of 10,000 times. The other, we give no crew and no goal. We start the engines and let it go. It will surely run itself up on the beach before it can get out of the harbor.

Our mind is standard equipment. Did you ever think that because your mind came to you free, you place little importance on it? Yet, the opposite is true.

Some Things to Think About

Whatever the mind of man can conceive and believe, it can achieve. Napoleon Hill

What a man can imagine or conceive in his mind he can accomplish. Impossibles are as impossible as thinking makes them so. Henry J. Kaiser

I am limited only by the thoughts I choose to encourage.
I have the power to select and control my thoughts.
I have nothing to deal with but my thoughts.
Present thoughts determine my future.
Thought is action, in rehearsal.

IF

If you think you are beaten, you are.
If you think you dare not, you don't.
If you like to win, but you think you can't,
It is almost certain you won't.

If you think you'll lose, you're lost,
For out of the world we find,
Success begins with a fellow's will—
It's all in the state of mind.

If you think you are outclassed, you are,
You've got to think high to rise,
You've got to be sure of yourself before
You can ever win a prize.

Life's battles don't always go
To the stronger or faster man,
But sooner or later the man who wins
Is the man who Thinks He CAN! ! ! !

7

Self-Image

The Self Image

What is this self-image and why is it so important? **Without question, the essential key to human personality and behavior is the self-image. Even our achievements are limited by how we view ourselves. If our self-image is altered, our behavior and personality are effected by the change.**

The self-image is the overall average of the various attitudes which we hold towards our capabilities in a multitude of areas. It is the "picture we have of ourselves." Our self-image, therefore, is of utmost importance because we cannot be any more effective, more successful, better coordinated, more creative or more anything other than what our self-image says we are. It is the *ceiling* on the *effectiveness* with which we can use our *true potential*.

The data in the subconscious mind governs the self-image and the self-image controls our effectiveness. It then becomes obvious that if we want to change our actions or attitudes, and thus change our behavior, we must add information to the subconscious that will reflect itself in our behavior.

35

Human beings are always changing and growing. They have an insatiable, never-ending need to better themselves. Around the self-image is built everything they do. It is the core of their being.

Behavior Dependent on Self-Image

Suppose we have a vertical line and calibrate it to represent bits of knowledge (the brain contains about 3 trillion facts of information by age thirty). We place an arrow at the top representing ever-increasing knowledge. Next we select a self-image in a certain area. This self-image is surrounded by an effectiveness range. Our performance is effective only within this range. This picture given to us by our subconscious tells us to a very fine degree just how we will perform. We can only act according to this picture. It is our comfort zone. Any performance outside this zone will produce tension.

The only way we can change our performance is first to change the self-image. It raises the ceiling on our effectiveness and allows us a greater use of our potential.

Better Self-Images Releases Ability

In order to change your self-image it is not necessary actually to improve yourself. It can be revised merely by repainting the *mind-picture* of yourself you carry in your imagination—your own private opinion and concept of that self. The change that comes from the development of a new self-image can produce rather fantastic results.

A person is usually more superior than he thinks he is. When he changes his self-image, he doesn't necessarily improve his skills and gifts. He only puts to use the talents he already possesses.

When Positive Thinking Will Not Work

The realization that you lack learning and wisdom is

36

the initial step toward acquiring them. Beginning to be a more proficient person starts when you first realize you are incompetent.

A fresh viewpoint has been discovered about the *power of positive thinking* which seems to answer why some people use it with success and yet others find it useless. When it is compatible with a person's self-image, *positive thinking* does undoubtedly function, but when it is incompatible with the self-image, it absolutely will not work.

As long as you hold any negative view of yourself, you will find it out of the question to think in positive terms.

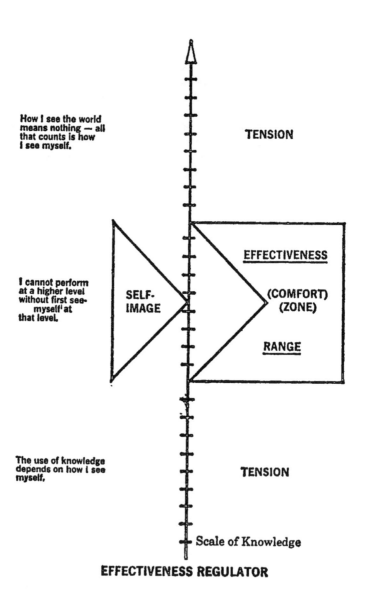

How I see the world
means nothing — all
that counts is how
I see myself.

TENSION

I cannot perform
at a higher level
without first see-
myself[i] at
that level.

SELF-
IMAGE

EFFECTIVENESS

(COMFORT)
(ZONE)

RANGE

The use of knowledge
depends on how I see
myself.

TENSION

Scale of Knowledge

EFFECTIVENESS REGULATOR

The essential key to human individual personality and behavior is the self-image. When the self-image is changed, everything else is affected.

38

How You View Yourself All-Important

How you look at the world means nothing. All that counts is how you look at yourself. Because how you look at yourself determines how you look at the world!

Everyone has the power to grow and to change.

What Makes You Good

Do you know what the largest room in the world is? It is the room for improvement.

Dizzy Dean, the great, big-league baseball pitcher, was asked why he practiced so much when he already was the leading pitcher in the world. He replied, *"When you stop getting better you stop being good."* This sums up the need for continued learning. The thing that makes you *good* is attempting to be *better*.

What We Think is True

Our behavior is controlled by what we think and believe to be true. The image we receive and store in our subconscious is not necessarily what is happening. We act according to what we believe is true.

Let us suppose, for example, that two men are walking on the trail—let's call them Bill and Jim. Jim tells Bill that he has sent their friend John further out on the trail dressed in a bear costume with the intention of frightening Bill. But he has decided not to let this happen; so he tells him about the bear costume and they continue on the trail until they reach the appointed spot. Meanwhile, unknown to them, John didn't show up, and a real bear was waiting!

What do you think were Bill's feelings when he saw the bear? Was he frightened?

Of course not, because he thought and imagined the bear to be John, and his emotional and nervous reactions would be consistent with this belief; so he reacted to what he believed to be true.

It follows that if our ideas and mental images concerning ourselves are distorted, then our reaction to our environment will also be inappropriate.

Again, the main key to individual personality and behavior is the self-image. The self-image limits what we can achieve.

Source of Ideas Unimportant

You must remember that it makes no difference how or by whom you have been programed with the various ideas you now have. No matter if they have been received from relatives, schooling, your friends—even from yourself— you are presently behaving in a manner based upon the belief that these ideas are true.

You have the ability, knowledge and potential capacity to perform whatever is necessary to attain a happy life of accomplishment and fulfillment. This capacity will be used by you as soon as you alter the beliefs that are inhibiting to you right now.

Inferiority

Feelings of inferiority are experienced to some degree by almost 95 percent of the world's population. To a major portion of these people, these feelings are a severe disadvantage in the attainment of fulfillment and satisfaction in life.

Inferiority feelings do not usually arise from actual experience, but from our own judgments and interpretations of events and experiences.

Inferiority complexes, which can intrude upon our lives, are developed from the feelings of inferiority that originate because we judge our performance and measure our abilities against someone else's and not against our own. When this happens, we will always be only a runner-up. When we evaluate our achievements by these criteria, we feel second-rate and unhappy. Consequently, we arrive at the erroneous assumption that we don't measure up.

Feelings of inferiority and superiority are conflicting feelings.

The plain reality is:

You are not *superior* to another person
You are not *inferior* to another person
You are merely *you*. Period.

A continuing feeling of inferiority soon deteriorates into an inferiority complex which causes a decline in the way a person performs. It is interesting to realize how this situation can be artificially created in a psychological test. Some kind of mean level of performance is set up, and then the test subjects are persuaded that they are below this average.

To illustrate this theory, a professor passed out a written test to his class, telling them that the normal time of completion was fifteen minutes. In reality, the test required about an hour to finish. After fifteen minutes, even the most brilliant students became upset, believing they were inadequate or mentally difficient.

Keep up with yourself. You are not in competition with anyone in this world.

Don't compare yourself and your performance with another person's accomplishments. You can never possibly attain *their* standards, nor can they attain yours. When you can unquestionably accept this truth as a fact and apply it in your daily life, your feelings of inferiority will evaporate.

Something to Think About

I'm not selfish. I'm simply deeply committed to me.

8

Definitions

It is necessary that we define certain words. These words when understood in the terms given will aid you in a better understanding of the subject.

PSYCHO-CYBERNETICS—"Self-steering" Helmsman or Steersman [from Greek] Method of steering, guiding or directing yourself toward a useful, productive, worthwhile, predetermined goal. (Positive Doing)

POTENTIAL—"Total knowledge" (innate plus experienced)

EFFECTIVENESS—"Degree of use of potential."

SUBCONSCIOUS—"Storehouse of Knowledge." (innate plus experienced) Vast unbelievable capacity to store knowledge. Controls all automatic body functions. Stores as memory all perceptions of the five senses.

SELF-IMAGE—"The picture we have of ourselves." Sets the boundaries of human accomplishments. The key to human personality and behavior. *How I look at the* *world means nothing. All that counts is how I look at myself.*

HABIT PATTERNS—"Automatic Response." (conditioned, without thinking)
1. Constructive (helps you reach your goals)
2. Restrictive (stops you from reaching your goal)
    a. Compulsive (have to)
    b. Inhibitive (can't)

PERSONALITY—"Outer expression of inner attitude or self-image." Something that attracts, and is obscure and inexplicable. Something that is freed from inside a person—easily sensed, but hard to explain.

DATA REVISION—"A direct and controlled method of changing the self-image." Method of programming experience, training response to high performance. Method to control input to control output. (G. I. G. O. Garbage in - Garbage out) Action in rehearsal.

ATTITUDE—"Habit of thought." Basic attitudes are formed up to seven years of age (formative years). Our success or failure is dependent upon these attitudes, yet we had no choice in their formation. The child starts out with an open mind and that is the last time he ever has one. He either becomes a bank president or a bank robber; or a diplomat who argues the question of the day or a pool shark who argues whose shot is next. In other words, he is either the victim or the beneficiary of these attitudes. It is our firm belief that a person does not have to go through his entire lifetime a victim of attitudes formed when he was a child—he can create attitudes that will get him the things he wants and help him reach the goals he sets for himself.

MOTIVATION—"The quality of human emotion that produces the drive that moves you to *action*" (Puts action in the doing).

Let's think of how people are motivated.

There is *incentive motivation* based on *reward* and *fear motivation* based on *punishment*.

An example of *incentive motivation* is the story of

43

the donkey being led by a small boy riding on a wooden cart down an unpaved country road. In his hand is a long pole with a rope tied on the end of it. A carrot dangles from the rope in front of the donkey's nose. The donkey then moves toward the carrot and pulls the cart—if he is hungry. This type of motivation eventually wears itself out, based on the need being satisfied.

An example of *fear motivation*—assume in the above story that the boy stops the cart at the side of the road and the donkey munches on some dry grass until his appetite is satisfied. What happens when he holds the carrot in front of the donkey? When the donkey doesn't move, the boy removes the carrot from the pole and commences to beat the donkey with the pole. If the donkey is afraid, he will move, but at some point will become immune. *While incentive motivation* and *fear motivation* both do work, there comes a time eventually when they do not produce the desired results.

What percentage of people in business today do you think are using either incentive or fear motivation, or both? Our premise is that an individual does not have to be lured with a prize or driven with a whip in order to accomplish anything. We believe a person can be moved by his own attitudes, which are lasting. This is called *attitude motivation* based on *change.*

The world is not short of people *who know how,* but it is in desperate need of people *who will do it.* They must, of necessity, put *action* into the *doing* rather than the *knowing.* People properly motivated will *go,* they will *move* and *do* things. It is the action idea of motivation that brings results.

No one gets far without motivation. Motivation is the number one need in achievement.

Since all action is based on *emotion* despite logic and reason, action itself springs from *feelings* and *emotions,* not from reason. Until the emotions are aroused there is no action.

The answer to becoming motivated and enthusiastic is simple—you must first be motivated toward something and be enthusiastic about something.

A person who has a goal and a plan to achieve it then develops the emotion needed.

44

Goal

Plan

Desire (increased desire for the goal)

Confidence (develops the confidence he can reach the goal)

Determination (finally he develops the determination that says, "I don't care what anybody says, thinks or does, I will reach my goal.")

SUCCESS—"Success is the progressive realization towards a productive, useful, worthwhile, predetermined goal."

It is necessary that you understand what success is. The dictionary defines success as "The accomplishment of a goal sought, a favorable outcome of something attempted, the attainment of wealth, fame and etc.", indicating that success is in the obtaining of something. In other words, this infers that when you do accomplish your goal you are a success, and therefore you are not a success until you do. However, defining success in these terms would mean that your success was only momentary.

We like to describe success as a *journey,* not a destination. When you are not actively progressing toward a goal, you are not successful. No matter how you measure success, no matter how much you attain of what you think you want, you will never arrive at a point called success. When you get where you think success is, you'll still find the road stretching invitingly ahead.

Success is related to potential.

Success is dependent on our effectiveness.

Simply stated, success is the result of attitude and habit. This places the attainment of success within the reach of everyone, because success attitudes can be developed and success habits can be formed.

Financial success is a rate of exchange of effectiveness. In business people earn money by providing products or services which are needed and useful. Financial success is not the result of earning money—earning money is the result of financial success.

HAPPINESS—"A state of mind when your thoughts are

45

pleasant most of the time" (happiness and success are synonymous). Happiness is a by-product of actively seeking a goal.

9

Do We See
What's Really There?

A very well-known quote from the Bible is, "Know the truth and the truth will set you free." This could mean that the truth that sets you free is the truth about *yourself*. Most of us underestimate ourselves and overestimate the problem. Now, what will this truth set you free of?—It will set you free from *fear*. Inhibition is always based on fear. Therefore, the only real freedom is being *free from fear*.

Examples

Many of the ideas and techniques we will review are as old as recorded history, thoroughly tested and proven. Some will be familiar, some many seem oversimplified and some may seem obvious.

Take your wrist watch and place it upside down next to you. Now write a description of the face of the watch. What kind of numerals does it have, color, second hand, dials, make, and any other details you can think of? Statisticians tell us the average person looks at his watch 5,000 times in one year. Multiply 5,000 by the number of years you've had the watch. Wouldn't you say that anyone who has looked at something that many times should know what it looks like? Let's see if you have described your watch. How many things did you leave out or get wrong? The reason is that you only look at your watch to observe the time. This makes the point—how many things do we look at and not really see?

Now try this . . . What does it say?

PARIS IN THE
THE SPRING

It does not say Paris in the Spring. Read it again. If you read it correctly, it will say "Paris in the the Spring." The third word "the" is repeated. Why didn't you see it? Because you have been conditioned not to see it.

TEST YOUR AWARENESS

First read the sentence enclosed in the box below

> **FINISHED FLIES ARE THE RE-**
> **SULT OF YEARS OF SCIENTIF-**
> **IC STUDY COMBINED WITH THE**
> **EXPERIENCE OF MANY YEARS.**

Now count the F's in the sentence. Count them only
once and do not go back and count them again.

How many did you get? Did you get three? That's normal. The correct answer is six. That's how many there are. Why did you miss them? Conditioning again. The sound of the "F" in "scientific" is different from the sound of the "F" in "of." One is an "F" sound and the other is a "V" sound. The result is that you block it out and you neglect to read it.

Read the following word:

What is it? Now concentrate on the white spaces instead of the black. It's "FLY", of course. Do we see what's really there? No, we can only see what we have been conditioned to see. We read black on white, not white on black. The thing that determines what we see is the assumption we have made when we look.

With the aid of the exercises in this book you will really be aware. You will then be able to see much more of what is really there. It will open up a whole new world for you and life will become more interesting and exciting.

Let's try a few more.

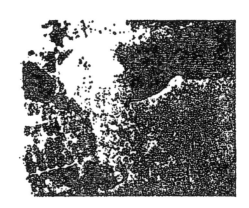

What do you see in this picture?

This is an actual photograph of a very familiar subject. It is not a trick or an illusion. We do not see this picture until our "minds" interpret what our eyes have seen.

What do you see with your eyes? All of the patterns of

49

experience and learning which have become a part of your unique individual mental process are involved in the complex act of perception. Even though your eyes see this photograph accurately in every detail, it will not have a meaning unless the various elements are correctly interpreted in the "mind." Yet, once you have seen it, you will wonder how you could have missed it.

Sometimes opportunities are like that—we look right at them and do not see them. One of the purposes is to increase awareness—of opportunity, of other people and of the ways in which you can use even more of your potential. Incidentally, the picture was the head of a *cow*.

A photographer took a picture of melting snow, with the black earth showing through the melted areas. It may

take you a while to see the face.* Once you see it, you may wonder how it was possible not to have recognized the person at once.

The picture is of Christ.*

50

What do you see
in this picture?

Do you see a young woman in a three-quarter view to the left? Or are you the one in five who immediately sees the old hag facing to the left?

In either case, you probably will find it very difficult to "turn off" the picture you first saw and reorganize its elements into the other figure.

This is a simple demonstration of how the mind tends to "lock on" to apparently satisfactory solutions to problems, blocking out alternatives and sharply curtailing creativity and *effectiveness*.

What does all this show us?

It shows that there is much more to our "image of reality." It shows that it is incomplete, inaccurate and there is *always more*. By being able to see and interpret more you increase your awareness and, consequently, your creativity. The more we see of what is really there, the more accurate is our view of reality.

> *"It isn't that you're stupid; it's that you understand so many things that just aren't so."*
> *"It's not what you don't know that harms you; it's what you know for darn sure that isn't so."*
> *"People don't think; they just think they think.*

What are they doing? They're reacting to what they think and believe to be true, they are reacting to past conditioning.

51

Victims or Beneficiaries

We are all bombarded constantly, from the day we're born, with limiting suggestions. You, at present, are either the victim or the beneficiary of ideas you were exposed to as a child.

Following are some examples of victims of erroneous ideas:

> **Opportunity knocks only once**
> **Born loser**
> **Not artistic (can't draw)**
> **Never could do anything right**
> **Children are seen, not heard**
> **Can't teach an old dog new tricks**
> **Clumsy kid (all thumbs)**
> **I'm not a business man (got "D" in geometry)**

The following paragraphs are *examples of conditioning:*

Circus Elephants and Limitations

An elephant can easily pick up a one-ton load with his trunk. Have you visited a circus and watched these huge creatures standing quietly tied with a light rope around one leg which, in turn, was tied to a small wooden stake driven several inches into the ground?

How was this accomplished?

While still young and weak, the elephant is tied with a heavy chain to an immovable iron stake embedded in several feet of concrete; no matter how hard he tries (and he does try) he cannot break the chain or move the stake. Then, no matter how large and strong the elephant becomes, he continues to believe that he cannot move as long as he sees his leg tied to the stake in the ground beside him.

The Pike and the Minnow

Picture a four-foot glass cube filled with water and a little minnow swimming around inside. The cube is divided in the middle with a glass partition. A pike is dropped in the water on the opposite side of the minnow. He makes an immediate dash for the minnow and, of course, he collides with the glass partition. After repeating this maneuver many, many times, the glass is then removed and he never again will try to attack the minnow.

These two stories will help illustrate the tremendous effect of conditioning by the process of repetition. When we are conditioned to believe something that isn't true, then our behavior becomes consistent with our belief.

There was a *Peanuts* cartoon by Charles Schultz in which one of the characters was spouting off about Charlie Brown and his lack of understanding of life and girls and even baseball.

She arrived at his house saying, "He plays a lot of baseball but I doubt if he even understands baseball." With that she knocked on the door and Charlie Brown put his head out. She said, "I don't think you understand *anything,* Chuck," turned around and walked away, leaving him standing with a blank expression on his face saying, "I don't even understand what it is I don't understand."

This is sort of an example of your dilemma. But you're *going* to understand what it is you don't understand!

10

The Process of Thinking

Hypothetical Analysis of the "Thinking Process"

The following is a hypothetical analysis of the "thinking" process. Science is rapidly coming to regard the "mind" and the "body" as separately acting entities. Actually, they are one complex interacting whole. Yet it is more convient to separate them and look at each area of activity. It is necessary to carry this a step further and look at three different parts of the mind in terms of the functions they perform for us. This is not the actual way they are divided, but our "thinking process" is. It is a hypothetical process and seems to explain the functioning of these entities.

We will divide this process into three functions, the *conscious*, the *subconscious*, and the *creative center*.

Conscious Mind

The part of the mind with which we are most familiar and, of course, of which we are most aware, is the conscious mind.

54

The chief functions of the Conscious Mind Are:

1. The *perception* of incoming information from the environment and from inside the person.

2. The *association* of current information about the environment and the functions of the body with part information or data which is in the memory files of the subconscious mind. (If the perception is of something not

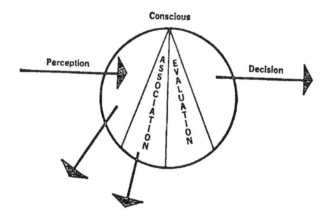

previously contained in the subconscious, the only function is to store this information.)

3. The *evaluation* of this association with respect to the best interest of the individual.

4. *Decision* and direction of action (or inaction.)

As you can see, each of us spends all of our waking hours running through these four steps: *Perception, Association, Evaluation,* and *Decision.* The process is exceedingly rapid, and perfectly accurate, based on the information. Only two things can lead to a decision, or action, which is not in the best interest of the person.

One is the failure to perceive something. This might happen because of failing eyesight or hearing, etc. The other possible reason for error would be inaccurate information or data, either from an external source or from the memory files in the subconscious The accuracy of the conscious mind, as with any good computer, is no better than the data available to us (G.I.G.O.—Garbage In Garbage Out.)

If the airline information clerk tells you on the phone that Flight 703 is scheduled to leave at 8:15 p.m., and you arrive at the airport at 7:45 p.m. only to find that the plane left at 7:15, then your directed action was wrong only because the data available was false. Many similar errors happen to us every day because of false data or the interpretation of this data in the remarkable memory storage files in the subconscious.

Subconscious

The Subconscious Mind has two primary functions:

1. It controls all the *automatic* functions of the body—such things as the beating of your heart, breathing, glandular secretions, etc. Even when the conscious mind is disconnected, whether through sleep, hypnosis or a concussion, the subconscious continues to operate automatically the various functions of the body.

2. It stores as *memory* everything that happens to the individual. And, as part of this memory storage capability, it is able to develop automatic or preprogrammed courses of action or thought which are called Habit Patterns. An important aspect of the subconscious mind is its inability to discriminate. It accepts inputs just as transmitted to it by the conscious mind. If the conscious view is distorted, then the recorded data will be distorted.

I AM VERY ACCOMMODATING

I ask no questions.

I accept whatever you give me.

I do whatever I am told to do.

I do not presume to change anything you think, say, or do; I file it all away in perfect order, quickly and efficiently, and then I return it to you exactly as you gave it to me.

Sometimes you call me your memory.

I am the reservoir into which you toss anything your heart or mind chooses to deposit there.

I work night and day; I never rest, and nothing can impede my activity.

The thoughts you send to me are categorized and filed, and my filing system never fails.

I am truly your servant who does your bidding without hesitation or criticism.

I cooperate when you tell me that you are "this" or "that" and I play it back as you give it. I am most agreeable.

Since I do not think, argue, judge, analyze, question, or make decisions, I accept impressions easily.

I am going to ask you to sort out what you send me, however; my files are getting a little cluttered and confused. I mean, please discard those things that you do not want returned to you.

What is my name? Oh, I thought you knew!

I am your subconscious.

By Margaret E. White

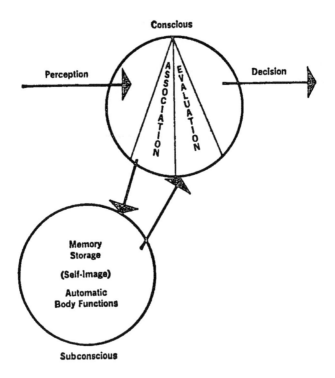

Conscious

Perception

Decision

ASSOCIATION

EVALUATION

Memory
Storage

(Self-Image)

Automatic
Body Functions

Subconscious

There is a two way communication between the conscious and the subconscious minds. Of course, the conscious is able to *transmit* information to the subconscious at will, whereas some of the bits of information in the subconscious are more readily available to conscious recall than others. Many of the memories which we have there are right on the surface, bits of information which we use all the time. We have an almost unbelievable scanning mechanism which is capable of looking over all of the available information instantly. Thus, we can tell immediately that a particular moving object is, for example, a new Chevrolet convertible, has two doors, is blue, has disc wheels and white wall tires, etc. If we had to go through each individual bit of logic and piece each bit of related information together consciously, it would take two to three weeks to come to the same identification. There are approximately ten billion memory cells in the human brain, each capable of storing 100,000 different bits of information. Every single thing that has ever happened to you is recorded there, every sight, every smell, every sound and every feeling that you have ever had since you were born, and, maybe a little before that. At age thirty the average person has accumulated about 3 trillion memories. (Of course, some of these memories have been repressed—blocked off from conscious recall).

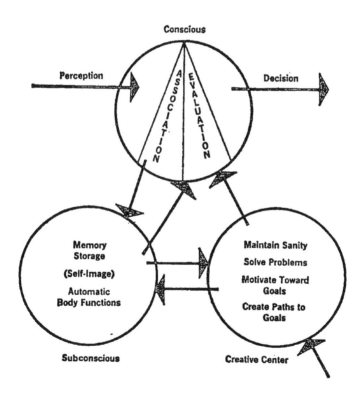

The Creative Center

There is the third mind—the Creative Center.

The functions of the third, and in many ways the most important, part of the mind are:

1. to maintain sanity.
2. to find creative solutions to problems.
3. to motivate the individual in the direction of his goals.
4. to develop new, creative means of achieving goals.

The Creative Center has only recently been recognized and researched. It has always functioned. Yet, specific methods by which the tremendous power of this section of the mind might be purposefully used have been developed only in the last twenty years.

When it is not used in a directive manner, the Creative Center functions automatically. It performs all four of the above operations whether or not you are aware of its existence, whether or not you direct it to do so. The maintenance of sanity is accomplished largely through dream therapy. The Creative Center is completely aware of all the pressures, tensions and emotional conflicts that are disturbing you. It is capable of reducing the effect of these reactions on your mental health by giving you a dream which is symbolic.

The finding of creative solutions to problems is equally automatic. How many times have you had a really serious problem on which you have worked for hours without finding the answer? Then, perhaps, you have laid the problem aside to take care of something else, only to have a perfect solution pop into your mind. Most people have this happen to them quite often. It is a perfectly normal operation of the Creative Center.

The third job of the Creative Center is motivation. When you have a properly defined goal (and we will talk about goals in detail later) the Creative Center does an extremely effective job of keeping you moving toward it. This does not necessarily mean that you will work harder. It does mean that you will work more intelligently and more effectively. It means that you will like the work which takes you toward your goal.

And, finally, the task of creating new means of achieving goals is the function of the Creative Center. It will supply the "means whereby" you will reach your goal. This is probably the most exciting function of the creative center—its ability to develop new techniques, new ways of doing things.

The solution to your goals may come from outside of your, giving you information that has not been previously recorded in your subconscious mind as indicated in diagram by outside arrow.

It has been proven through experiments by Dr. J. B. Rhine of Duke University that a human being has available to him certain facts and knowledge other than what he has stored in his subconscious.

11

The Secret of
Creative Thinking

Original thoughts and ideas are not conceived at the conscious level, but come out of the subconscious, seemingly "out of nowhere." When the conscious mind has freed itself from the question, and is actively thinking about something else, creative ideas emerge. However, they do not materialize without first giving some conscious thought to the problem.

First, a person must be concerned with seeking a solution in order to activate an "inspiration." One should consciously gather all the facts of the situation, and weigh the possible alternatives. Then, after analyzing the problem and mentally picturing the most satisfactory outcome, it is necessary to relax and allow one's subconscious imagination to go to work.

Conscious effort is the greatest impediment to effective creativity. When you use conscious effort, you restrain and prohibit your automatic success mechanism from working.

It has been shown that when you try to use will power or effort of any kind to change your beliefs or to correct bad habits, there is a negative rather than a positive result.

Deliberate effort is one of the major factors in a person's falling short of his goal.

In his "law of reversed effort," Emile Coué said, "When the will and the imagination are in conflict, the imagination invariably wins. . . ."

Other scientific discoveries showed that effort is one of the main forces prohibiting a person from discontinuing a bad habit or acquiring a new one. It has been found that a habit is, in reality, strengthened when a person makes an effort to curb it.

Physical relaxation, when practiced daily, brings about an accompanying mental relaxation and a "relaxed attitude" which aids us to consciously control better our automatic mechanism.

The Human Mind's Potential for Creative Ideas

The potential of the human mind for creating new ideas is unlimited. Everyone's subconscious mind is a *storehouse* of thousands and thousands of *stored facts*—and these facts can be combined in an endless variety of combinations to create endless numbers of ideas.

When the mind comes up with a *creative idea,* it has selected two or more separate facts that were unconnected and flashed their relationship to conscious level.

When you need an original answer to a specific problem, no matter in what area of endeavor—whether in business or the arts—you must have a desired end result in your mind. Even if this result is obscure and indefinite, you will recognize it when you come upon it.

The main consideration is to apply yourself as diligently as possible, feeding into your subconscious all available information on the subject. Then, if you allow your creative success mechanism to go to work, it will automatically sift through the data available and will come up with a solution to your problem. Sometimes, when you least expect it or when you are thinking of an entirely unrelated

63

subject, your conscious mind will take over and you suddenly realize you have the answer.

EXAMPLE: The following four facts were existing separately and unconnected in a person's mind:

1. Six months ago he saw an obscure news item in the local paper stating that the county was going to surface the roads in the area bounded by Black Canyon Road, Glendale Road, Bell Road, Carefree Road.

2. A week ago he learned that the 100-acre Butler Farm was for sale. (The farm is within the area mentioned above.)

3. He is aware that ABC Corporation is planning a new plant in town and will hire 3,000 new employees.

4. He recently went house-hunting with his son (for his son and his family). He found there was an acute housing shortage.

It is easy enough to see the relationship of the above four facts now that they are put together. Now they suggest a money-making real estate opportunity, such as:

Buy Butler Farm—now easily accessible over improved roads—and sell it as a real estate development to house the new employees of the ABC Corporation plant.

The mind, in order to develop this relationship and produce the *idea* had to choose these four facts from among thousands.

All of us need some kind of discipline that will start the unconscious mind into its creative process (servo-mechanism). An essential part of creativity is *not being able to fail.*

Nothing is new—and everything is new. It's a matter of

exposure and *absorption*. It is what your mind does with what funnels through your five senses.

In your search for originality and creativity, remember, it requires no special genius—what you need is:

OBSERVATION   RETENTION   SELECTION

Age has little to do with it—ideas come from "young minds." It's not how *old* you are, but how *bold* you are.

ACCUMULATION (collect-amass-increase)	*Stack up on facts*
CEREBRATION (function of the cerebrum-act of thinking)	*Ponder on it*—let the tongue of your mind taste it and toss it around "upstairs".
GESTATION (development of idea or plan in the mind)	*Let it work & wait* (mental oven) The subconscious takes over and stews over it. (You stop thinking)
ELATION (feeling of success)	*You've got it—you've struck oil!* The idea starts gushing.

Success Mechanism

You have within you a mechanism which will locate a goal automatically, when this goal has been previously set by you. To illustrate this goal-seeking mechanism, sit at a table blindfolded and have someone set a small object within your reach. First your job will be to locate this object. You will do so by a trial and error method until you finally locate it. Then, after picking it up, replace it exactly where it was originally placed, leaving the blindfold over your eyes. Now sit back in your seat, reach out and pick it up.

Let's review what happened here. When we set out to locate the object, we made a number of errors, each time possibly saying to ourselves, "No it isn't there," until we finally located it. We did not relate the errors or mistakes as failures. In the second attempt you undoubtedly reached out and touched it on the first try. You forgot the errors and recorded the success by creating a picture of it. This picture led you to your target.

Something to think about

When the will and the imagination are in conflict, the imagination always wins.

The greatest hindrance to effectiveness is conscious effort.

12

The Quiet Place

Marcus Aurelius said:

"Men seek retreats for themselves; houses in the country, seashore and mountains; and you, too, are wont to desire such things very much, but this is altogether a mark of the most common sort of man. For it is in your power, whenever you shall choose to retire into yourself. Constantly then, give to yourself this retreat, and renew yourself."

Need for Finding a Peaceful Retreat

It is necessary for every person to have a peaceful place within himself to which he can retreat for self-renewal. This place should be completely isolated from the outside world. Everyday stress and tension can cause frayed nerves and can cause him to be upset. A quiet place should be available to him to restore his serenity. He needs to go to it at least once a day, in order to calm himself and to revitalize his inner strength.

Construct in Your Imagination

Teaching oneself the art of seeking out the quiet center is one of the most well-received ideas we have ever suggested to our students. The easiest way to retreat into this quiet center is to mentally construct it in your imagination; to plan, build, paint and decorate it according to your own taste and preference so that it will be comfortable and attractive to you. You must truly feel "at home."

When you create a place where you can be alone with yourself, you are escaping from reality. It is necessary for you to shield yourself and be free from the daily attack of outside distractions. Everyone needs an occasional vacation, a change of scene to get out of a rut and away from daily obligations.

When you retreat into your *quiet place,* your nervous system gets a rest every day. As you mentally do this, a feeling of freedom takes over and calmness and peace will come over you. This tranquility will undoubtedly carry over into any actions that follow. The quiet time will literally clear out the cobwebs and free you for new and challenging activities.

It is not outside events that are your key to being agitated or calm, but your own response to the things that happen around you.

Harry Truman's Quiet Place

It is important that we have a place in our minds that we can relax. Harry Truman claims to have had such a place. He referred to it as "a foxhole in my mind where I allow nothing to bother me." He would retreat into this foxhole in his imagination when anything bothered him.

What Is It?

It can be a sort of a retreat strictly of your own making,

68

a secret place somewhere where you will be perfectly safe, all alone—a room with mystical, if not magical qualities. It can be furnished simply or luxuriously—soft chairs, special pictures on the walls. A hi-fi stereo with a complete collection of the world's music, and even a very sophisticated computer that can solve any problem. It can be a small house on a quiet beach on an unchartered island in the Pacific dotted with palm trees and a light breeze blowing the waves ashore. The house may have a picture window taking in this whole view, or it can just be on a cloud, or deep in the earth or on a distant planet millions of light-years away. Don't tell anybody where your quiet room is. You are the only one that knows. Nobody can go there but you. This is the atmosphere where you are anything you care to be.

How Long To Arrive

Just close your eyes and recall the last time you were in San Francisco, New York, Chicago or out in a park. Did you get a picture of the Golden Gate Bridge, Fifth Avenue, Michigan Boulevard or the trees and greenery in the park? It takes just an instant to get to any of those places in your imagination. That's how long it will take you to get to your secret place. It's that simple.

Practice Exercise

Go to your quiet place at least once a day for relaxation and renewed energy.

13

Relaxation

We are convinced that "stress" does not have to be an accepted part of the world we live in.

Our lives could be much more serene and carefree if we would only recognize that God has given each one of us a built-in success mechanism which allows us to live as successful individuals. We create and compound our own problems when we force ourselves to employ conscious thought in finding the solution to complication which intrude on our lives.

As we have mentioned previously, you could compare your creative success mechanism with an electronic brain or high-powered computer. Your forebrain is the operator feeding data and problems into the computer which, in turn, is unable to *create* anything. Its job is to recognize the problems, sort out the data and relate to them. It was never designed to solve problems. Therefore *you* must not try to solve them with conscious effort.

The Art of Relaxation

If you happen to be traveling through a good, smooth period of living, then allow yourself to *feel* happy. Go the limit to sense the cheerfulness and pleasantness of the present moment.

John A. Schindler, M.D., has said, "Good emotions are the best medicine and the greatest power for good health. The physiological effects of good emotions are just as great in the right direction as the effects of bad emotions are in the wrong direction. Healthful living is more a matter of having the right kind of emotions than anything else. It is then apparent that the most important aspect of living consists in training and handling our emotions."

He has given us a few simple rules that will help us make our lives richer.

Keep life simple. Be responsive to the simple things near at hand—get your pleasures from the world that lies immediately before your five senses. Then life becomes a tremendously interesting adventure.

Avoid listening for the knock in your motor.

Learn to like your work.

Have a good hobby.

Like people.

Make a habit of saying the cheerful, pleasant thing.

Meet your problems with decision.

Be Consciously Aware of Your Environment

You should attempt to develop a more conscious awareness of your surroundings; to what you are presently responding and reacting in relation to your five senses.

A highly-developed awareness and understanding of what is going on *right now* will actually help you to reduce tension. When you find yourself tightening up, ask yourself this question:

"What is there in my present environment right now that I am able to react to in a positive way?"

71

The function of your creative servo-mechanism is to develop the appropriate response *right now* to your immediate environment. If you are not aware of your reactions you will continue to react by habit to some other event out of your past. If you react in this manner, you are not responding to what is going on now, but to that past event.

Actually you are reacting to a possibility, not to a reality. When you have understanding of the situation this knowledge can often effect an overwhelmingly instantaneous remedy.

Relaxation is Learned

Relaxation is an acquired talent—like driving a car, sewing, hitting a baseball, cooking and selling. It is necessary that you relax in order to allow the automatic success mechanism to work. Relaxation tends to cut off the conscious mind and to accelerate the subconscious mind.

Relaxation is a way of immunizing yourself against external disturbances by refusing to respond to them.

Psychological Relaxation

Let us review four vital aspects of psychological relaxation:

1. **Forgive yourself**
2. **Forgive others**
3. **Keep up with yourself (not others)**
4. **See yourself at your best**

If you find yourself tensing up, check on the four vital rules and see if you are not breaking one or more of them!

Practice Exercise

Begin each day a new and better way by reciting the following:

72

This is the beginning of a new day.
I have been given this day to use as I will.
What I do today is important,
because I'm exchanging a new day of my life for it.
When tomorrow comes, this day will be gone forever,
leaving in its place whatever I have traded for it.
I pledge to myself
that it shall be for gain, good, and success,
in order that I shall not regret the price I paid for this day.

My thinking and my attitudes are calm and cheerful.

I act and feel friendly toward other people.

I am tolerant of other people, their shortcomings and mistakes, and I view their actions with the most favorable understanding possible.

I act as though attainment of my goals is sure to happen. I am the kind of individual I aspire to be, and everything I do and the way I feel expresses this individuality.

I will not allow my judgment or attitude to be affected by negativism or pessimism.

I try to smile as often as possible; at least several times a day.

I respond in a calm and intelligent manner without alarm, no matter what the situation.

If I cannot control a situation, I try always to react in a positive manner, even to negative facts.

I know that if I apply myself to forming habits to enable me to act in the above manner, it will have a positive influence on my self-image in a most constructive way. By making these actions a part of my life, I will notice a definite growth in my self-confidence.

**READ THE ABOVE EVERY DAY FOR
TWENTY-ONE DAYS**

14

The Psychology of Goals

There is no real happiness, no sense of achievement or contentment in life if a person has no goals to accomplish.

Move Forward

When you are moving forward, you are able to correct your course as you go. Your automatic guidance system cannot guide you if you are standing still.

You have a real sense of direction when you are able to concentrate on your goals. When you have this sense of direction, when you're looking toward something, you maintain your balance. When you have no personal goals which mean something, you may go around in circles, and feel lost and purposeless.

Energy To Reach Goals

First, in order to cause our goal-seeking mechanism to operate, the goal must be within the scope of the self-image. Second, the greater the desire for the goal, the more smoothly and energetically the *machine* will function. The creative center will be stimulated to provide the necessary "means whereby" for realizing the goal and to supply whatever energy is needed. The person who drags out of bed in the morning and limps through the day has goals way below his potential. His creative center is barely working. Even though the energy is there, the goals are so low that very little energy is needed.

The man who always seems to have an unlimited supply of creative energy has learned to set goals at a higher limit of his potential. The higher the goal, the higher is the self-image expressing itself. Aim high, rather than low, and you will become energetic and creative.

Goals Should be Consistent, Compatible, and Constructive

Each goal should be *consistent* and *compatible* with others, in other words, you don't set a goal of a $250,000 home while earning $10,000 a year. Make it a harmonious picture and blend them together to form the complete picture.

Your goal should also be *constructive,* a goal which is high enough to stimulate the creative center. Set goals at the outer edge of your self-image. For example, a man driving a 1967 Ford does not set a goal for a 1968 Chevrolet. On the other hand, he doesn't decide on a chauffeur-driven Rolls Royce, either.

It is just as wrong to set a goal so low that you can reach out and have it without any effort at all as to set one so far beyond your present self-image. In either case it would have no stimulating effect whatsoever. If you can almost believe it possible, but not quite, then it is high

75

enough. Sometimes people fall into the trap of setting a goal so inconceivably high that they don't bother reaching it.

"Goals by the yard are hard—Goals by the inch a cinch."

Set intermediate or short range goals to reach long range goals. Short range goals are more believable, while long range goals are more meaningful, but you must, in both cases, *clearly see the end result*.

The Ant and The Straw

A story that illustrates all this work we are about to do is comparable to the story of an ant and a piece of straw.

A biologist tells how he watched an ant carrying a piece of straw which seemed a big burden for it. The ant came to a crack in the earth which was too wide to cross. It stood for a time, as though pondering the situation, then put the straw across the crack and walked over upon it.

What a lesson for us! The burden becomes the bridge that will aid you in reaching any goal.

Why do men with goals succeed and those without fail? Involved in goal-setting is the Secret of Success. The key to success and failure is, "We become what we think about," or, "As a man thinks, he is." When a person is thinking of a productive, useful, worthwhile, predetermined goal, he absolutely succeeds. The things that are important to you that you really want should fill your thoughts.

"Imagination is more powerful than knowledge." Get an image in your mind of where you want to go and keep it there. Think of where you want to go, not where you don't want to go.

How Do You Do This?

First you must select your goals. As already mentioned, your basic goals have already been determined. There are *no others*—they are all categorized under these four headings:

Security (Physical Emotional Financial)
Love
Ego Satisfaction
Bodily Comforts and Possessions

It is the degree of these desires that makes people unique.

Security—the assurance that we are guarded against the hazards and dangers of life. This implies the protection of self and the desire for safety, health, food, clothing, shelter and preservation of a long life.

Love—the assurance that we are loved and we can safeguard our loved ones. This implies protection of loved ones and includes sex, romance, marriage, parenthood and family.

Ego Satisfaction—the inner assurance that, as individuals, we are to be admired and are capable of winning admiration. This implies protection of one's feelings and includes respect, approval, importance, appreciation, pride, prestige, recognition, status and personal satisfaction.

Bodily Comforts and Possessions—the provision of a life standard that will assure physical satisfaction. This means the acquiring of material things that can be bought with money; such things as conveniences, luxuries, a home, a car and physical surroundings of ease and beauty.

They determine what is important to you and what you think is important determines your actions.

Two Reasons Why People Do Anything

There are only two reasons why an individual does anything. They are:

1. to gain a benefit (something he does not have).
2. to avoid a loss (something he now has).

If it would be possible for you to consult all the sociologists and anthropologists who study people in groups, all the psychologists and psychiatrists who study individuals, or any other human behavioral scientists, you would find that they cannot come up with one single additional reason why an individual does anything.

The process of living becomes very simple when you understand that man has only these four basic goals and only two reasons why he does anything.

A human being always acts, feels and performs in accord with what he imagines to be true about himself and his environment. This is a basic fundamental law of mind. Your selection will determine how you wish to satisfy these goals.

For example: No one needs a $10,000 car, when a $2,000 car will get him where he wants to go. The $10,000 car satisfies a need other than transportation.

For example: If you have a home that performs the basic need of security, then you have satisfied this need. However, wanting another home that is larger and more elaborate, surrounded by things of ease and beauty, you are satisfying a need for respect, approval, importance, recognition and prestige, or *ego satisfaction.*

Set up your present goals under these four headings. Remember—the degree of the intensity that you desire these things defines what is important to you.

How Can You Appraise
Your Chances For Success?

What can you do to improve your chances and exploit your opportunities? What you *do* tells a lot, but *why* you do it tells even more. What you want out of life is significant, but how hard you work to get what you want is even more significant.

Look for signs of "motivation" in your ambitions, attitudes and the way you feel about yourself, your job and everything you have done or plan to do. "Good motivation" is probably your most important quality and the lack of it is a most serious drawback.

Have you been enthusiastic in attacking opportunities in the past? What do you get excited about and why? Do you get a real kick out of doing things well? Do you take advantage of time off? What have you done to broaden yourself, to think more and to be more useful? What do you get out of your learning experiences? What have you made out of your opportunities? Are you goal-oriented? Do you make plans? How specific? Do you have the ability to communicate? Can you put your thoughts across in writing or in words? Do you have leadership ability?

The only real gauge you have to judge motivation is *what has moved you in the past and what you have your eye on for the future.*

Get yourself a goal or a series of goals. Get yourself a project. Determine what you want out of life. Never stop looking ahead toward something that will bring you satisfaction and happiness. You will find when you're not looking forward, not actually striving toward a goal, you're only existing, and not really *living.*

Again, no one can feel really happy or content if he tries to exist without goals to accomplish.

I'M SATISFIED WITH MYSELF, BUT THE FEELING ISN'T MUTUAL.	I'D TRY TO KNOW MYSELF BETTER, BUT I DON'T WANT TO GET INVOLVED.
Figure 1.	*Figure 2.*

Figure 1. Who is saying these words? The man in the mirror or the man outside the mirror? The man in the mirror represents the self-image, therefore, he is not satisfied with the man outside, because there is always room for improvement.

Figure 2. The only way you can improve your self-image is to get involved with yourself.

Something to think about

Goals need desire.
Goals provide motivation and enthusiasm.
Goals create awareness of opportunities.
Specifics give direction.
Men of accomplishment seldom reach their goals; their goals keep moving ahead of them.

15
Goals

The purpose of the following eight steps is to help you analyze yourself and help you determine your goals. When you have completed these, you will have a good idea of what your goals are today.

1. Following is a list of ten areas in which you will rate yourself. The degree of the liabilities shown in this exercise determines the need for a goal.

	Assets (degree of use)	Liabilities (degree not used)
a. Ability to earn money	_____%	_____%
b. Leadership ability	_____%	_____%
c. Work ability	_____%	_____%
d. Getting along with others	_____%	_____%

e. Sports and hobbies   _____%   _____%

f. Family relationships   _____%   _____%

g. Persuasion ability   _____%   _____%

h. Memory (ability to recall) _____%   _____%

i. Awareness of potential   _____%   _____%

j. Confidence   _____%   _____%

For the above exercise fill in the Asset column from 0 to 100, then subtract this figure from 100 to get the Liability. (Don't spend much time thinking about this. Your subconscious will provide the answer.)

2. After this exercise is completed you will develop a *composite self-image* rating by totaling your ten asset scores and dividing by ten.

a. _____%

b. _____%

c. _____%

d. _____%

e. _____%

f. _____%

g. _____%

h. _____%

i. _____%

j. _____%

Total _____% ÷ 10 = _____%

This is my composite Self-Image rating.

3. Next you will arrive at the things you need right now. If we offered to give you anything you wanted, what would you choose?

Suggestions: new furniture; car repair; new clothes; dental work; medical insurance; new refrigerator, etc.

I need the following:

_____ _____

_____ _____

_____ _____

_____ _____

_____ _____

The above items you would list if we offered to write a check for anything you had listed. Don't be hesitant to write everything that comes to your mind.

4. This will help you arrive at the personality qualities you need in relation to the goals you have set.

Suggestions: ability to concentrate; real personal confidence; to be more aggressive; to finish what I start; more original creativity; to be friendlier to others; to be a leader; to be in good health; to be enthusiastic; to react calmly; to organize my time; to have a good memory; to be more diplomatic; to be goal-oriented.

I need and want the following:

_____   _____
_____   _____
_____   _____
_____   _____
_____   _____

5a. PERSONAL CHARACTERISTICS TO BE ACQUIRED

Greater use of *potential* (knowledge)

Understand myself better

Understand other person better

More *alert* (to opportunity and new ideas)

More *tactful* and *diplomatic*

Get along with others better (handle people skillfully)

Better health (maintain good emotions)

Think clearly and accurately

Communicate more effectively

More *aware*

Friendlier person

Better *memory* (recall)

More *tolerant*

More *aggressive*

More *relaxed*

More *goal-oriented*

Enjoy my work

Be a happier person

5b. Now analyze some of your personal characteristics that help you arrive at your goals.

Concentration	Speech
Imagination	Reading
Efficiency	Emotions
Courage	Relaxation
Self-confidence	Decisiveness
Self-respect	Maturity
Self-organization	Composure
Self-liking	Interest in People
Self-starter	Planning
Self-education	Accomplishment
Self-discipline	High Quality in Work
Time-organization	Motivation of Others
Perseveranse	Calmness
Creativity	Cheerfulness
Energy	Enthusiasm
Memory (Recall)	Communication

6. Analyze the feeling of "I Can't."

a. Is there some job or some particular duty you would like to perform, but feel that you can't?

b. Ask yourself why you can't.

c. Do you base your inability to perform on real truth, or just on what you assume to be true?

d. Do you have a real reason for believing this to be the truth?

e. Could you possibly be mistaken in your belief?

f. Would you hold the same belief in the situation applied to someone else?

g. If what you believe is not the truth, why do you continue to act in this manner?

Because we have so many memories of past failures,

and unpleasant experiences in our subconscious does not mean they have to be "dug out," exposed or examined to effect a personality change.

If you are constantly reminded of your former blunders, you will likely find it difficult to change your behavior pattern. Remembering these past mistakes tends to have a detrimental effect on your actions. When you continually remind yourself of them, you are, not using your power of reason.

It is certainly not logical to conclude that because you may have failed once you are doomed to failure again.

To say to yourself, "I can't" before even trying and in the absence of evidence is certainly not rational. Your answer should be like the man who, when asked if he could play the piano, replied, "I don't know, I have never tried."

These past failure experiences do not harm you as long as your conscious thought is centered on what you do want, not on what you don't want.

7. Fill out your personal balance sheet.

PERSONAL BALANCE SHEET OF:

	Assets (degree of use)	Liabilities (degree not used)
KNOW-HOW Total experience, knowledge, formal education, training, developed talents (Ability to perform)	_____%	_____%
ENERGY Physical drive (physical health) Ability to work at top efficiency	_____%	_____%
TIME How you organize it, make it work for you, ability to properly use it. How efficiently you use it.	_____%	_____%

IMAGINATION
Creative spark
Ability to foresee and solve
problems. (picturing power of
the mind)   _____%   _____%

PEOPLE
Family, friends, business associates (how they help you)
Knowledge of human relations
behavior   _____%   _____%

RESEARCH AND DEVELOPMENT
Investments of time and/or
money in improving perfor-
mance in all areas of living   _____%   _____%

8. ANALYSIS TO BE USED IN THE SELECTION OF GOALS

Answer the following questions YES or NO.

LEADERSHIP
1. Should people have to pay school taxes if they do not have children?
2. I try to see what others think before I take a stand.
3. I would rather have people dislike me than look down on me.
4. I must admit I am a pretty fair talker.

INTELLECTUAL EFFICIENCY
1. Do I read at least ten books a year?
2. When faced with a problem, do I find I act on impulse to solve it?
3. Do I like science?
4. Do I feel teachers often expect too much from their students?

AMBITION
1. Do I always try to do a little better than what is expected of me?
2. Did I like it very much when one of my papers was read to the class in school?

3. Do I believe that in many ways the poor man is better off than the rich man?
4. Do I believe that planning my activities in advance is likely to take the most fun out of them?

RESPONSIBILITY
1. Do I feel that when prices are high I can't blame someone for getting all he can while the getting is good?
2. Do I feel every family owes it to the city to keep its sidewalks cleared of snow in the winter and its lawn mowed in the summer?
3. Do I feel we ought to take care of ourselves and let everybody take care of themselves?
4. Do I feel any guilt or shame if I fail to vote in the elections?

CONVICTION OF SUCCESS
1. Do I think there are as many opportunities for an ambitious person as there ever were?
2. Do I often have doubts as to what action will win approval for me in my work?
3. Do I doubt that I will ever be an important person? . . . that I will make a real contribution to the world?
4. Do I get nervous and upset when I feel I have been placed in competition with another?

The answers to these questions are at the end of this chapter.

Self Analysis Questions

The self-analysis questions on the pages that follow will serve as a guide and a stimulus in arriving at your goals in each of the six most important areas of your life.

SOCIAL	**MENTAL**	**FAMILY LIFE**
SPIRITUAL	**PHYSICAL**	**FINANCIAL**

These self-analysis questions are merely stimulative. They are by no means the only questions you are to ask yourself, but they are designed to start you thinking in the right direction. You will then see an amazing thing happen. These questions will quickly suggest other thoughts, ideas and other questions in each area of your life that will give you the correct goal to pursue.

If you are too close to achieving your objectives, you need to set higher goals. If the attainment is too far away, you need to set up intermediate steps. Remember— "Success by the yard is hard, but by the inch is a cinch."

These questions will aid you in setting more "challenging" goals.

SOCIAL DEVELOPMENT
1. Do you consider yourself very sociable? Moderately sociable? Antisocial?
2. Do you get along with your children?
3. Do you genuinely like people?
4. How many people have you invited into your home in the last three months?
5. Into how many homes have you been invited in the last three months?
6. How many times have you gone out with friends in the last three months? At who's invitation—yours or theirs?
7. Do you look forward to parties and social affairs? Are you more anxious to have guests in or to be invited out?
8. Do children make friends with you quickly? Slowly? Or not at all?
9. What is your general attitude toward "society?" Are you objective? Optimistic? Pessimistic? Indifferent? Resigned? Completely unaware?
10. Do people seem to like you? What can you do to make them like you more?
11. In social affairs do you consider yourself a leader? A follower? An average participant? Which would you like to be?

SPIRITUAL DEVELOPMENT
1. Do you consider yourself a religious person?
2. Do you adhere rigidly to your moral or ethical standards?

3. Do you modify your beliefs to allow free expression?
4. Do you practice flexibility by deciding right or wrong on the merits of each situation?
5. Do you ever make decisions based on axioms, proverbs or "wise sayings" you learned during your childhood?
6. Do you count among your close friends any people you consider to be spiritually sound?
7. Do others come to you for counsel or advice? How many in one year? Are you able to help them?

MENTAL DEVELOPMENT
1. How do you consider your intelligence level? Above average? Average? Below average?
2. Do you consider your learning rate to be fast? Average? Slow?
3. What was the extent of your formal education?
4. If you could turn the pages of time back would you extend your education to a higher level?
5. What supplemental training have you had in your present field?
6. What training or refresher courses have you taken in the last five years?
7. What steps have you taken to complete your mental development?
8. Do you consider your education and training to be well-rounded?
9. To what magazines do you subscribe?
10. What types of articles interest you the most?
11. Have you a strong desire to know more?
12. Are you embarrassed because you know so little?

PHYSICAL DEVELOPMENT
1. Do you consider your state of health excellent? Good? Fair? Poor?
2. Are you the outdoor type?
3. How many days have you lost from work in the last 5 years due to health? What was the length of each absense? Cause of illness?
4. When did you have your last physical check-up?
5. Do you have a regular program of seeing your doctor, dentist, and optometrist?

6. Are you a weight-watcher? What foods do you enjoy? Dislike?

FAMILY LIFE DEVELOPMENT
1. Was your childhood home a close family unit? Did you do things as a family? Did you really enjoy them?
2. How does your present family life compare or contrast with what you experienced as a child?
3. Do you reserve time for your children?
4. Do they ask your opinion about personal problems or decisions?
5. Who makes decisions in your family—husband or wife?
6. Who decides where the family will go on vacation?
7. Do your children invite their friends to your home?
8. Do you have certain "home rules" of conduct that are clearly established to recognize the rights of the individual.

FINANCIAL DEVELOPMENT
1. Do you consider your income to be average? Above average? Below average?
2. Is your spending compatible with your earnings?
3. Has your income increased yearly?
4. Do you have a regular savings program?
5. Do you regularly make up a personal financial statement?
6. Do you have an operating budget?
7. Have you ever dreamed of inheriting a large sum of money? Was it specific? What was it? What would you do if you received this amount?
8. Do you have an insurance program?
9. How do you evaluate your present worth to your present job? Are you paid what you deserve? More? Less?
10. What can you do to increase your worth?

Something to think about

Goals need desire.
Goals provide motivation and enthusiasm.

Goals produce awareness of opportunities.
We move toward that which we dwell upon.

ANSWERS:

LEADERSHIP
1. Yes
2. No
3. Yes
4. Yes

INTELLECTUAL EFFICIENCY
1. Yes
2. No
3. Yes
4. No

AMBITION
1. Yes
2. No
3. No
4. No

RESPONSIBILITY
1. No
2. Yes
3. No
4. Yes

CONVICTION OF SUCCESS
1. Yes
2. No
3. No
4. No

Each correct answer is 25 points—grade yourself.

16

Synthetic Experience

Revising Data in the Subconscious Mind

The principle of affirmation (a statement of belief) has been known and utilized for as far back as recorded history. It has been used by schools of religion and philosophy. Only recently have we had a functional understanding of why the repeating of an affirmation has had such a dramatic effect on a person's behavior.

Nothing Succeeds Like Success

It is a direct and controlled method of changing the self-image; we learn to function successfully by experiencing success (nothing succeeds like success). Our memories of past successses are our stored information which give us the self-confidence for our present position. But how does a person draw on memories of past successful experiences when either he has had no experience or he has experienced only failure? His dilemma is comparable to the man who cannot secure a job because he has had no experience and cannot get the experience because he can't get a job.

Human Nervous System
Cannot Tell The Difference

Clinical psychologists have proven experimentally that it is impossible for the human nervous system to distinguish between a real experience and one created in the imagination. (The brain waves of the real event are the same as the imagined.) This provides us with a very potent and effective tool.

Successful affirming requires three things:
Desire   **Information**   **Repetition**

The Time to Recondition the Subconscious

There are many times during the day when revising the data in the subconscious is effective. Basically they are any time when you can be thoroughly and completely relaxed and *be aware of only your thoughts*. These are the times when the communication channel with the subconscious flows most freely—immediately upon awakening in the morning (when you are still in an unaware state, unmindful of anything except your thoughts); just before you fall asleep at night; immediately after returning from lunch or at any other time you are alone and can relax.

The first step in making an *affirmation* is to take the goals analyzed from the previous eight steps, and then make a written explanation (for yourself) of why you want to acquire a particular goal or personality trait. In other words, describe it to yourself in as much detail as you can (Descriptive Statement). Then prepare a simple *Statement of Affirmation,* the purpose being to help you create clear mental pictures.

When you are in a relaxed state (physically and mentally) repeat this statement in your imagination and form a mental picture of yourself performing appropriately.

94

Then sense the emotional feelings that are a result of having performed accordingly.

Begin by knowing you have arrived.
Words   Pictures   Feelings

If you are wondering whether you go through all three phases each time you are attempting to revise the data in your subconscious mind, the answer is an unqualified "yes."

In using this technique it is important that you stand aside and let it work. Revising the data by using this technique brings results. *Let it work. Don't try hard to change. Don't continually check your progress.*

Just let it happen; especially don't talk about it with other people. Do not predict the things that are going to happen to you. Just quietly use this technique and you will feel the changes soon enough or, possibly, your friends will begin to notice the change. That will be time enough for discussion.

Determining Words For Affirmation

The following are rules and suggestions for choosing the words used in an affirmation:

1. Be strictly personal. Use *I, me* or *my.*
2. Be absolutely positive - move *toward* what you want; avoid the words *not* or *don't.*
3. Use the present tense.
4. Do not be progressive.-Avoid *I am going to.*
5. Do not be comparative. Never compare with the *past* or *others;* do not use *more than* or *better than.*
6. Avoid the words *able to* or *can.*
7. Affirmation should be balanced. *Do not use opposites or extremes.*
8. Be realistic. *Do not use absolutes or perfection.*
9. Always write for yourself, *not for others.*

10. Do not set time limits. *Time limits are deadly; they create tension.*

You Supply The Goal

Your automatic creative mechanism functions according to the goal you set. Once you give it a definite objective to achieve, you can depend upon its automatic guidance system to take you to that objective much better than you ever could by conscious thought. Your automatic mechanism will supply you with *how* you will reach your goal.

IF YOU DESIRE TO IMPROVE YOURSELF
REMEMBER THIS FACT.
ACT THE WAY YOU WANT TO BE (IN YOUR IMAGINA-TION). AND YOU'LL BE THE WAY YOU ACT.

Check List to be Used in the Writing of a Descriptive Statement.

1. Do I "really" want this? (This must be something I "really" want, not something that will "sound" good if someone else reads it.)
2. Is the goal compatible with my other goals?
3. Is it positive? (State what I want, not what I want to get rid of.)
4. Is it expressed in "total" detail?
5. Is it realistic? (Is it possible for some human being to achieve it? Not just, "Is it realistic for me today?")
6. Is my goal high enough?

Reach out! Set the goal limit high. Nothing should enter my mind at this point as to how I will achieve these goals.

7. Am I including personality factors necessary to achieve my goals?

96

An example of a Descriptive Statement:
I want to be able to speak in front of a group of people, but I seem to lack confidence that I can do this. I am always nervous and fearful that I will make a mistake or forget something. I know if I can build confidence to do this, it will rub off in other areas, especially in my job.

I can see myself giving a talk on creative thinking in front of about 200 people. I'm an expert on the subject, because I know more than anyone present. I'm standing on the rostrum, and as I give my talk, the audience responds with applause and appreciative laughter. At the conclusion, as I leave the speakers' platform, several key people offer me congratulations, giving me a feeling of importance and self-esteem.

Affirmation: **I AM A CONFIDENT SPEAKER.**

Something to think about

Whatever you vividly imagine, ardently desire, sincerely believe, and enthusiastically act upon, will inevitably happen.

Creative Wording and the Subconscious

We are going to consider only words, written and spoken, and their effect on you. Your subconscious responds to your words, especially when they are repeated over and over again. It takes your words literally—it cannot reason like your conscious mind.

Case History

The following case history demonstrates the use of creative wording showing a bad or negative result.

A person was going to a doctor for headaches. The doctor had prescribed many drugs for the relief of pain, but as time went on the person did not react to the drugs and consequently did not get rid of the pain. We had a conversation which uncovered the cause of his headaches.

During the first half hour of discussion it was particu-

97

larly noted that he frequently used the phrases, "that gave me a headache" and "he gave me a headache." He was using creative wording to give him a headache, and it created a real one for him. His headaches were caused *only* by his repeated statements that these things or people gave him a headache.

This man was actually using his subconscious to work against him. He soon realized that the repetition of such statements actually did create the end results. He now knew he could get help from the subconscious to do anything he wanted to do. He only had to use words that would give him the end result he wanted. Your mind is so powerful, it will give you exactly what you want once you understand the method of getting it.

Actual Physical Manifestation

Here are some examples that are often used and are converted into actual physical manifestations.

> I get tired of . . .
> I can't see . . .
> . . . gives me a pain
> I can't stomach that
> I can't swallow that
> I'll be damned
> . . . drives me crazy
> . . . makes me sick
> . . . gives me a headache
> I can't stand . . .
> . . . gives me a pain in the neck
> . . . gets under my skin

Become Aware of Words

When you say things like these, your subconscious is being conditioned to what you say. Beginning right now, become aware of the words you use. Examine what you say and think, and all that is said to you. Remove these words or phrases from your vocabulary and become aware when they are said to you. Replace them with something that will bring good results.

Case History

One day a young man came to me with a desire to be in one of our Psycho-Cybernetics Workshops. He explained his predicament. He had no money and he was hopelessly in debt (he thought) and deeply depressed. He was unmarried and his mother lived with him. He owned an art shop in Scottsdale, Arizona, in which he featured his own work as well as the works of other artists. He was a very talented sculptor with a very bad "self-image." We agreed to have him attend the Workshop Sessions after having him make two promises: first, that he would attend all the Workshop Sessions and do all the techniques and exercises prescribed; secondly, that he would pay us when he was able.

When we were working on Data Revision, he made six affirmations:

1. The art shop would be sold at a figure sufficient to pay all of his debts.
2. He would be released from his house.
3. He would have a place for his mother to live.
4. He would have $10,000.00 in the bank.
5. He would have freedom from financial worries and time to sculpt.
6. He would fulfill a desire to travel.

When he had completed several weeks assuming in his imagination that these things had already taken place, he came to me one evening and said, "I must be going crazy because I'm experiencing happy feelings and my situation has not changed one bit." I told him what he was experiencing was change, and when this change had taken place inside he then would experience what he had been affirming.

This is exactly what took place. All six of his affirmations became a reality within six months.

This case is not as unusual as it seems. He owes this success to his discipline in following the techniques and exercises prescribed in this book.

Case History

One day a furniture designer described her difficulties in working with a prominent manufacturer. She was convinced that he unjustly criticized and rejected her best work and that often he was deliberately rude and unfair to her.

Hearing her story, it was explained that if she found the other person rude and unfair, it was a sure sign that she, not the manufacturer was in need of a new attitude. She had learned that the power of this law of assumption or data revision and its practical application could be discovered only through experience; that only by assuming that the situation was what she wanted it to be could she bring about the changed desires. Her employer was merely bearing witness, telling her by his behavior what her concept of him was. It was suggested it was quite probable that she was carrying on mental conversations with him in her mind which were filled with criticism and recrimination. There was no doubt that she was mentally arguing with the producer, for *"others only echo that which we whisper to them in silence."*

She confessed that every morning on her way to work she told him just what she thought of him in a way she would never have dared address him in person. The intensity and force of her mental arguments with him *automatically established his behavior toward her.* She began to realize that all of us carry on mental conversations. Unfortunately on most occasions these conversations are argumentative; that so many people are mentally engrossed in conversations and few appear to be happy about them. The very intensity of their feelings must lead them to the unpleasant incidents that they themselves have mentally created and therefore must now encounter.

When she realized what she had been doing, she agreed to change her attitude and to live this law of assumption

100

faithfully by assuming that her job was highly satisfactory and her relationship with the manufacturer was a very happy one. She would follow the method prescribed and *imagine* that he had congratulated her on her fine designs and that she, in turn, had thanked him for his praise and kindness. To her great delight she soon discovered for herself that *her own attitude* was the cause.

The behavior of her employer miraculously reversed itself. His attitudes, echoing, as it had always done that which she had assumed, now reflected her changed concept of him.

What she did was by the power of her imagination, her persistent assumption, influenced his behavior and determined his attitude toward her. This is one way we can see it is not facts, but our *imagination by which we create and shape our lives.*

17

Mental Picturing

All through the ages, philosophers, scientists and various teachers of religious principles have been constantly confronted with a major question:

How can we reach the human mind
with a major truth that will set it free?

When they had achieved the answer to this question, it seemed that all they would have to do would be to tell people about the new life that was open to them, and everyone would be naturally anxious to try it. But experience indicated and proved the contrary. The mind of man has always opposed change with a strong intensity; it does not welcome progress. When the human mind has been provided with the actual power that could set it free, it has used various evasions, rationalizations and oppositions which have prevented it from accepting the truth.

Teachers of the truth did come upon a method, and it worked. It enabled people to take charge of their own lives. They received great inner strength. They solved their daily problems and physical difficulties became a thing of the past. As each new day appeared, it became fresh and meaningful to them. They became calm, and a

whole new self-image developed.
What was this method?
The method was the mental picture.

Advantages of Mental Pictures

1. Everyone understands a mental picture.

2. Everyone has the ability to form mental pictures and to draw meaning from them.

3. A mental picture is a scene played upon the "screen of the mind." Its value is extensive. The thinking process itself is largely a projection of mental scenes.

4. The mental picture gives the mind a positive course of action to follow.

5. It provides a powerful and accurate guidance system.

6. It guides the individual into doing what is necessary to reach a goal.

7. It creates the mind as to a positive course of action to follow.

8. We can all understand a mental picture that illustrates an idea.

9. The picture becomes the bridge that helps us reach the unknown.

10. It connects one level of understanding to a higher level of understanding.

11. We move up from a literal understanding to a psychological understanding.

12. A mental picture, once implanted, works ceaselessly and effortlessly.

13. When a mental picture is absorbed, it begins working immediately.

14. It transforms our thinking and supplies energy and wisdom even when we are not consciously aware of it, working quietly, giving us whatever we need to reach our goal.

This wonderful "secret" was known and practiced by all the great teachers of the *truth*.

Result of Mental Picturing

We have come to a greater understanding, through the science of cybernetics, of the reason mental imagery yields such astounding results. They are not produced by the supernatural or trickery, but are effected by the spontaneous and instinctive workings of our brains and intellects.

The brain and nervous system, together, are regarded as a cybernetic device or a complicated *servo-mechanism*. It is an involuntary machine which *directs* itself toward its goal-target by using negative feedback based upon stored data, shifting its course when necessary.

An example is a self-guided missile, with a predetermined target. When it is traveling on a correct course (positive feedback) it actually needs or gets no direction; it continues on its way and does not react to positive feedback. When it gets off its course (negative feedback) it does respond to the information that reaches its mechanism, telling it, for example, that it is off its path too far to the left. The corrective device automatically causes the steering mechanism to veer back to the right. While doing this, if it *overcorrects*, it will then steer back to the left. The missile reaches its goal by moving forward, making mistakes and constantly correcting them. It makes a series of zigzags, finally arriving at its target.

The important thing for us to note is that when it was on a failure course, it did not consider this a *failure*, it kept moving forward and correcting its course.

TARGET   START

The straight line is the shortest distance between the release of the torpedo and its goal. The zigzag is the path the torpedo actually follows, always moving towards its goal.

The reason mental pictures are so significant is that

104

fully 83 percent of what we perceive is through the sense of sight.

Create a Mental Picture

This letter describes a rather complicated accident that supposedly occurred to a bricklayer in the British West Indies. It makes humorous reading. Follow along and create the mental pictures:

Dear sir:
When I reached the construction site I found that the hurricane had knocked some bricks off the floor of the main building.

So I rigged up a beam with a pulley at the top of the building and hoisted up a couple of barrels full of bricks. When I had repaired the building, there were some bricks left over.

I hoisted the barrel back up again and secured the line at the bottom, and then went up and filled the barrel with extra bricks. Then I went to the bottom and cast off the line.

Unfortunately, the barrel of bricks was heavier than I and, before I knew what was happening, the barrel started down, jerking me off the ground. I decided to hang on, and halfway up I met the barrel coming down and received a severe blow on the shoulder.

I then continued to the top, banging my head against the beam, getting my fingers jammed in the pulley. When the barrel hit the ground it burst out the bottom, causing all the bricks to spill out.

I was now heavier than the barrel and so started down again at high speed. Halfway down, I met the barrel coming up and received severe injuries to my shins. When I hit the ground I landed on the bricks and received several painful cuts from the sharp edges.

At this point I must have lost my presence of mind, because I let go of the line, and the barrel came down, giving me another blow on the head and putting me in the hospital.

I respectfully request sick leave.

Your servant,
Ricardo

Something to think about

Your mental picture of yourself is the strongest force within you.

Hold a picture of yourself long and continuous in your imagination and you will be drawn toward it.

Picture what you want - not what you don't want.

18

Think Sheets

This book has been designed to increase your abilities in many areas of human endeavor. Perhaps one of the most important areas of improvement will be a tremendous increase in your ability to visualize your goals in preparation for their accomplishment.

All of the puzzles that will be given to you are of a purely logical nature as distinguished from riddles. They will contain no plays on words, no deliberate deceptive statements and no guessing. In short, no "catches" of any kind.

The puzzles are of a completely non-mathematical nature, requiring thought and mental imagery. That is, they will use native mental ingenuity which utilizes the store of acquired information you already possess.

It is interesting to observe that solving puzzles of the purely logical type epitomizes the scientific process of reaching your goals as stated in *Psycho-Cybernetics*. At the onset one is confronted with a mass of more or less unrelated data. From these facts a few positive inferences can be drawn immediately, but it is usually necessary to set up a clear picture in your mind of just what your goal is. For in reaching your goals, as in solving these puzzles, a knowledge of the feeling of victory will be your greatest asset.

As you solve these puzzles you will find that you are calling upon many of the mechanisms you use in reaching your goals. In both cases inconsistencies will appear. Your success mechanism will be called upon to reject negative assumptions and substitute positive affirmations until a consistent set of conclusions—a clearly defined goal—emerges.

We reflect on the fundamental processes of rejecting negative influences and reinforcing positive affirmations, drawing conclusions from them, and examining their consistency (within the framework of the problem at hand). Thus, the solution of the problem, as it is with the achievement of our goals, is ultimately brought about from the mass of seemingly unrelated information initially provided. So it is in science, too.

A great mind once said, "When learning ceases to be fun, it ceases to be learning." To this end we present the following THINK SHEETS.*

It is inherent in the nature of logical puzzles, as in the achievement of our goals, that the solution cannot be reduced to one fixed pattern for all.

Think Sheet No. 1

CONSIDER THE FOLLOWING:

1. Having to catch a 6:00 a.m. flight, I woke up while it was still dark. Not wanting to wake my wife, I went to the closet to get a pair of shoes and socks without putting the light on. I found my shoes and socks, but I must confess they were in no kind of order—just a jumbled pile of 6 shoes of 3 brands and a heap of 24 socks, black and brown. How many shoes and socks did I have to take with me into the bathroom to be sure I had a pair of matching shoes and a pair of matching socks?

2. We are watching the midnight news on Channel 4 and the weather man says, "It is raining now, but we can expect the storm to pass in 72 hours, at which time it will be a bright, sunny day." What is wrong here?

3. A contest was held with three contestants, one of whom was a graduate of the Psycho-Cybernetics Seminar

* Reprinted, with permission, from the book "HOW TO RAISE YOUR I.Q." by Sheldon Howard.

and Workshop. The moderator made this statement to all three contestants:

"Every pain has been taken to make this a perfectly fair contest, as all three of you will be given exactly the same information at every point of the contest."

At this point the three competitors were blindfolded. A white piece of paper was taped to each one's forehead, and they were told that not all of the pieces of paper were black. The blindfolds were removed and the prize was to go to the first man to correctly deduce whether the paper on his forehead was white or black and write his answer on a sheet of paper out of the view of the other two contestants.

The Psycho-Cybernetics graduate wrote his answer immediately while the other two contestants took two minutes to solve the problem. All three wrote "white." How did our Psycho-Cybernetics graduate come to his conclusion so quickly?

4. At the local bank the positions of cashier, manager and teller are held by Brown, Jones and Smith, though not necessarily respectively.

1. The teller, who was an only child, earns the least.

2. Smith, who married Brown's sister, earns more than the manager.

What position does each man fill?

Think Sheet No. 2

1. When was the most recent year that reads the same upside down?

2. A tramp rolls cigarettes from the butts he picks up on the street. He finds that four butts make one new

cigarette. How many cigarettes can he smoke from a haul of sixteen cigarette butts?

3. I always sit in the same pew at church; the third from the front and the seventh from the back, on the right hand side. Each pew seats five persons on each side of the center aisle. What is the total capacity of the church?

4. A lady bought a hat with a floral decoration for $10. If the hat costs $9 more than the decoration, how much did the decoration cost?

5. A non-stop train leaves Los Angeles for San Francisco at 6:00 p.m. traveling at a constant speed of sixty miles per hour. At 7:00 p.m. the same day a freight train leaves San Francisco for Los Angeles at a constant speed of forty miles per hour. Los Angeles is 400 miles from San Francisco. How far apart are the trains one hour before they pass each other?

6. A boy has as many sisters as brothers, but each sister has only half as many sisters as brothers. How many boys and girls are in the family?

7. Bob, Paul, Richard, and Sam are four talented, creative artists; one a dancer, one a painter, one a singer, and one a writer (though not necessarily in that order).
1. Bob and Richard were in the audience the night the singer made his debut on the concert stage.
2. Both Paul and the writer have posed for portraits by the painter.
3. The writer, whose biography of Sam was a bestseller, is planning to write a biography of Bob.
4. Bob has never heard of Richard.
What is each man's artistic field?

Think Sheet No. 3

1. I asked my math teacher to sell me a copy of his new book. He said he would for this amount:
"Put two silver dollars in front of a silver dollar, and

two silver dollars behind a silver dollar with one silver dollar in the middle."

What is the least I would have to pay?

2. If a salesman and a half can sell an order and a half in a day and a half, how many doctors will six salesmen sell in seven days?

3. Three women each have two daughters, and they all get on the bus to go shopping. There are only seven empty seats on the bus, but each has a seat to herself. How did they manage it?

4. A doctor in Los Angeles had a brother in San Diego who was a lawyer, but the lawyer in San Diego did not have a brother in Los Angeles who was a doctor. WHY?

5. My daughter put a dime in an empty wine bottle, then replaced the cork and challenged me to remove the dime without breaking the bottle or taking out the cork. How can this be done?

6. I happen to notice at exactly the moment of low tide a boat tied to a buoy at the local marina. A rope ladder was hanging over the side with ten rungs a foot apart. The bottom rung was just visible above the surface of the water. The water will rise eight feet at high tide. How many rungs of the ladder will be visible at high tide?

7. Two lawyers were both defending a young man in a civil action regarding a contract for the purchase of a used car. One of the lawyers was father to the son of the other lawyer. How could this be true?

8. If I drive at an average speed of thirty miles per hour from my house to the Railroad Station, I just catch the train. On a particular morning there was a lot of traffic and at the exact halfway point, I found that I had only averaged fifteen miles per hour. How fast must I drive for the rest of the way to catch the train?

Think Sheet No. 4

1. A twelve-inch phonograph record is recorded from the outer edge to two inches from the exact center, while a seven-inch phonograph record is recorded from the outer edge to one inch from the exact center. (Each record is recorded on one side only). The twelve-inch record revolves at thirty-three revolutions per minute and plays for fifteen minutes while the seven-inch record revolves at forty-five revolutions per minute and plays for three minutes. How many more grooves on the twelve-inch than the seven-inch record?

2. The math teacher said to the student, "I have looked over the twenty-five test papers you have turned in this year, and I can't make up my mind whether to give you an "A" or "B". You are right on the borderline. However, I will give you the "A" if you can solve this problem: I'm giving you back all of your test papers and six paper clips. Fasten an odd number of papers with each paper clip, with no papers or paper clips left over." The student got his "A." How did he do it?

3. I weigh ninety pounds plus half my weight. How much do I weigh?

4. If I can build a square wall around a one-acre lot with 12 truckloads of bricks, how big a square lot can I enclose with a similar wall containing twenty-four truckloads of bricks?

5. Mr. White, Mr. Black, and Mr. Green were having lunch together. One was wearing a white tie, one a black tie and one a green tie. The man wearing the white tie noticed that each was wearing a tie matching the names of the three men. Mr. Green agreed and also noticed that none of them was wearing a tie that matched his own name. What color tie was each man wearing? Is there enough information given to solve this problem?

6. Bob, John, Harry and Chuck all work for Apex Inc. as clerk, foreman, supervisor and manager. All are paid in whole numbers of dollars.

The manager earns twice as much as the supervisor.

The supervisor earns twice as much as the foreman.

The foreman earns twice as much as the clerk.

Bob does not earn more money than Harry, and Harry does not earn twice as much as Bob, yet Bob earns $10,753 per year more than John. What position does each hold?

7. Two trains are thirty miles apart. They start toward each other at fifteen miles per hour and as they start, a fly takes off from one train toward the other at forty miles per hour. As soon as the fly reached the other train, he reversed his direction and headed toward the first train. He repeated the process of flying back and forth at a constant rate of speed until the trains met. How far did the fly fly?

Answers
Think Sheet No. 1

1. Three socks, four shoes.
2. It will be midnight again.
3. Every pain . . . etc.
4. Brown is the manager, Jones is the teller, Smith is the cashier.

Think Sheet No. 2

1. 1961
2. Five
3. Ninety
4. .50 Fifty cents.
5. One hundred miles
6. Four boys and three girls.

7. Richard is the writer; Bob the dancer; Paul the singer; and Sam the painter.

Think Sheet No. 3

1. Three silver dollars ... $3.00
2. Total of twenty-eight orders.
3. One is a woman, who has two daughters, each of whom have two daughters.
4. The doctor in Los Angeles was his sister.
5. Instead of taking the cork out, just push it into the bottle.
6. Ten rungs.
7. The other lawyer was his mother.
8. It was too late, I had already missed the train.

Think Sheet No. 4

1. No more grooves in the twelve-inch than the seven-inch. They both have one groove.
2. Use one clip on each group of five sheets. Then clip the total together with the sixth clip.
3. I weigh 180 pounds.
4. Four acres.
5. Mr. White was wearing a green tie. Mr. Black was wearing a white tie. Mr. Green was wearing the black tie.
6. John is the clerk. Bob is the foreman. Chuck is the supervisor. Hary is the manager.
7. Forty miles.

19

Imagination

Imagination is more important than knowledge.
- - - - - - - - Albert Einstein

Certain words have taken on so many strange meanings and connotations in the course of time that they almost cease to have any meaning whatsoever. One such word is "imagination." This word seems to serve many ideas—some of which are even directly opposed to another. The word imagination has such a wide variety of uses and so many diverse meanings, it really has no fixed significance.

For example, when we say to a man, "Use your imagination," we mean his present outlook is much too restricted. Next we suggest to him that his ideas are "pure imagination" implying his ideas are unsound. When we refer to a jealous or suspicious person we say, "He is a victim of his imagination," meaning his thoughts are untrue. Therefore, the word imagination seems to have no definite meaning.

The dictionary defines imagination as, "The picturing power or act of the mind; the process of forming mental images of the objects of perception or thought in the absence of concrete external stimuli; the mental ability to reproduce the images of memory; the reproductive faculty of the mind."

Imagination is said to be "the gateway to reality." By our imagination we have the power to do or be anything we desire. If we realize this we then realize that only as we live by imagination are we "truly living" at all. *It is the inner world of continuous imagination that is the force which will make it happen in the outer world.* It enlarges the vision, stretches the mind, and challenges the impossible. It projects your thoughts in search of creative achievement. You must firmly implant in your mind a picture of the person you want to become with all of the benefits and advantages this stature will bring you. See yourself winning the admiration and respect of your family, friends and business associates.

Our success mechanism is activated by our imagination which has given us a picture of our goal. A common misbelief is that action is taken, or we fail to act, because of will power. The real source is our imagination.

A person's behavior, actions and feelings are based upon what he imagines to be the truth about himself and everything around him. This is an elementary and essential mental law.

It is impossible for the nervous system to distinguish between a real experience or one created in your imagination. What you *believe, think* and *imagine* to be the truth will determine how your nervous system responds.

Hold this image constantly in your mind. It will transform your outlook on life. It will spur you on to further study and thought, generating within you an unquenchable enthusiasm, a zest for a fuller and richer life, and motivate you to do the things necessary to attain it.

Something to think about

Before imagination can flow, you must let go.

116

20

The Method

Ten minutes each day should be reserved for sheer relaxation. During this period you should be by yourself and without distractions. Now, with your eyes closed, start to *exercise your imagination.*

Vivid Imagining

The mental pictures which you create in your imagination should be as close to actual experiences as you can make them; as lifelike and as complete in every detail as possible. This can be accomplished by becoming aware of and by focusing your thoughts on all the minute particulars that you perceive with your five senses. (For all reasonable intentions, details relating to the environment are extremely vital, because if the experience you create is intense enough, your nervous system will accept it, the same as a real one.

Imagine Yourself Successful

During this ten minutes that you envision and feel yourself performing in a natural way, your past actions are unimportant. It doesn't really make any difference how you behaved on another occasion. It isn't essential to be absolutely confident and behave in an entirely satisfactory manner. Your nervous system will accept the fact eventually, if you imagine yourself the way you want to be. Picture yourself already as you would like to be. How do you feel? If you have behaved in a tense and unsure manner, imagine how you would feel if you were acting in a calmer manner, more intelligently and with more assurance.

Concentrate Imagination on Goal

Concentrate your attention upon the *feeling* that you already are that person. The great secret is a *controlled imagination and well-sustained attention*. Firmly, repeatedly focus on the goal to be accomplished. Suppose you could not afford a trip; that your financial status would not provide for this. Would imagination be sufficient to produce this goal? Suppose you are capable of acting with continuous imagination and capable of sustaining the feeling of this goal as already accomplished. Will your assumption in your imagination produce the fact? Is your imagination a power sufficient, to assume the feeling of the goal already accomplished? Is it capable of producing the reality of this idea?

Experience has convinced us that an assumption (though false) if persisted in, will produce the goal; that all our reasonable plans and actions will never make up for our lack of continuous imagination.

Concentrate Imagination Objectively

A word of caution. We use our imagination correctly, not as an onlooker (objectively), but as a *participant* (subjectively). *We actually must be there in our imagination.* This is not mere fantasy, but a truth you can prove by experience. Every goal is already there as a mere possibility as long as you *think* of *it,* but is *overpoweringly real if you think from it.*

Determined imagination, thinking *from* the end result is the beginning of all miracles. We would like to give you belief in miracles, but a miracle is only the name given it by those who have no knowledge of the power and function of imagination.

The Future Becomes the Present

The future must become the present in the imagination of the person who wisely and consciously creates the circumstance. We translate vision into *being* when we are thinking *from* instead of thinking *of.* This, reason can never do. By its very nature it is restricted to the senses, but imagination has no such limitation. Through imagination, man escapes from the limitation of the senses and the bondage of reason. There is no stopping a man who can think *from* the end result. It does not matter what he has been or what he is, all that matters is *what he wants,* because he knows by use of his continuous imagination his assumptions will harden into reality.

This inner journey into imagination must never be without direction.

Man attracts what he is. This is a firm law of the universe.

"Man attracts to himself that which he sets out from himself."

The art of living consists in sustaining the *feeling* of your goals as *already being fulfilled* and letting things come to you.

Only Now Counts

It is only what is done *now* that counts. The present moment does not recede into the past, as so many people commonly believe. It advances into the future to confront us.

A Great Truth

When man discovers that his world is his own mental activity made visible, then no man can attract to himself anything other than what he has set out in his imagination.

It was a momentous day when we realized this great truth: *that everything in our world is a manifestation of the mental activity that goes on within us;* that the conditions and circumstances of our lives only reflect this.

Therefore, practice frequently *in your imagination* the feeling that your goal has already been fulfilled. This is creative magic, and in this way you become the master of your fate.

When you understand this function of the imagination, you hold in your hand the key to the attainment of all your goals.

The truth that sets you free is, "You can experience in your imagination what you desire to experience in reality, and by maintaining this experience in your imagination your desired goal becomes a reality."

Increase Attention on Feeling

The success of this method is to focus your attention on *feeling* that your goal has already been fulfilled, without permitting distractions. All of your progress depends on the *increase of attention*. The ideas which move you to action are those that dominate your consciousness and possess your attention.

To the unenlightened this may seem like fantasy, yet all progress comes from those who do not accept the world as it is.

When you set out to control your attention, you then will realize how little you actually presently control your imagination and how much it is dominated by the five senses.

Go Forward With Imagination

"Man either goes forward in imagination or remains imprisoned in his senses."

Controlled Attention

Your imagination is able to perform in direct proportion to the degree of your attention. Attention is attracted from outside of you when you are consciously aware of external impressions. It is directed from within *when you have chosen deliberately what you will be preoccupied with mentally.* There is a great difference of thought attention directed objectively and subjectively. This control is achieved when you concentrate on the thoughts you have deliberately predetermined. You will no longer be dominated by outside circumstances and conditions.

To help you create more control, here is a practice exercise. Just before you fall asleep at night, attempt to hold your attention on the day's activities in reverse order. Place your attention on the last thing you did—getting into bed, and then go backward in time to the first thing you did—getting out of bed. This may not be the easiest exercise, but remember, just as specific exercises help develop specific muscles, this will help you develop the muscles of your "attention." Your attention must be developed, controlled and concentrated in order for you to affect a successful change in your self-image and your future.

Principle of Least Action

You must imagine yourself experiencing your goal as already being achieved, together with the accompanying "feeling." You attain deliberate conscious control of your imagination.

"Begin by knowing you have arrived."

This method employs the principle of "least action" which governs everything in physics. Least action is the minimum of time multipled by minimum of energy. The *future* becomes the *present* when you imagine you are or already have what you have assumed in your imagination. You then assume the "feeling" of possession of these things.

Actions Are Automatic

This is a method of revising data in the subconscious mind which controls your nervous system. After you have practiced this for twenty-one days, you will find yourself behaving differently, without conscious thought or effort.

Now you do not have to try in order to feel insufficient and inadequate because you have stored up in your subconscious mind memories created by faults, both real and imagined. These memories generate your feelings of ineffectiveness automatically for you.

These actions have come about from the negative thoughts programed into the subconscious. Conversely, this method will work just the same on positive thoughts and thereby will create a new *self-image*.

Conscious Not Responsible For Results

A person decides upon an objective with conscious thought. Then he gathers all the data, he evaluates it, and finally reaches a decision. The final outcome of this decision is allowed to take its course. (See diagram on page 58.)

Points For The Successful
Use Of This Method

Essential:
1. A strong desire for whatever it is you want (goal).
2. Cultivate the physical state of immobility described. You must learn to induce this state at will. The greater energies of the mind are available only when the body is still and the door to the senses is closed.
3. Experience in your imagination the "feeling" of already having achieved your goal. Experience daily for 21 consecutive days.

Law Works Impersonally

One of the prevalent misunderstandings is that this law is workable only for those who have a devout or religious principle. This is definitely a fallacy. It works impersonally, just as the law of gravity or electricity.

How To Utilize The
Power of Rational Thinking

Your automatic success mechanism is completely detached and disinterested. It performs much like a computer operating from data in the subconscious mind, creating for you the proper feelings to complete predetermined goals. It functions on data with which you have programed into your subconscious in the form of thoughts, views, convictions, evaluations and impressions.

Our future and present are not decided by constantly turning over and reviewing the past. When a person does this he becomes obsessed with underlying emotional problems which do not allow him to remember or to regulate and direct his present thoughts.

IN THE THEATER OF MY MIND

At night, upon my bed, my eyes closed tight,
  I inward glide, collecting scattered thoughts to reap,
And reassemble as a script desire did write,
  To be performed upon the imaged stage of sleep,
entertaining GOALS. While affirmations wing in flight
  Thru thin, pale scenes of thought my visions keep.
To hear, to see, to touch, to be what ere I might,
  Creates a play, with props from fancies formless heap.
          And the Hero is me.
What fleeting, filmy feelings will my mind achieve,
  As senses, with my dream fulfilled are sate?
What if this inward drama I do then believe,
  And store within my heart, and calmly wait?
Then in a way, tho surely one I can't conceive,
  One day, that dream will be my waking state.
And when I know a web of life that I did weave,
  I'll also know that I controll my fate.
          My dream and I are free.

                              H. J. Halverson—
                              a psycho-cybernetics student

Something to think about

  Imagination is more important than knowledge.
  Man attracts to himself that which he sets out from himself.
  Man goes forward in imagination or remains imprisoned in his senses.
  Begin by knowing you have arrived.
  Take imagination and enthusiasm and hitch the two together. Then fix your gaze on the farthest star and forget about the weather.
  You can experience in your imagination what you desire to experience in reality and by maintaining this ex-

*perience in your imagination, your goal becomes a reality.
Before imagination can flow, you must let go!*

Introduction to Rod Serling's Twilight Zone:

"There is a fifth dimension beyond that which
is known to man. A dimension as vast as space
and as timeless as infinity. It is the middle
ground between light and shadow beyond science
and superstition and it lies between the pit of
man's fears and the summit of his knowledge.
This is the dimension of imagination."

21

How to Make Use
Of Negative Feedback

Glance at Negatives,
but Concentrate on Positives

The instrument panel of any modern feedback system contains negative indicators in the form of light panels which become illuminated when anything goes wrong. If this happens, it does not mean that the system is defective, but merely an indication that steps should be taken to correct the problem. If the signal is disregarded, the mechanism may be damaged. When one of the panels lights up, no one becomes upset.

However, it is not necessary to give the instrument panel one's undivided attention. An occasional glance at the negative indicators is all that is required. There is no need to concentrate on them, and major attention is focused on the positive aspects of the mechanism.

How To Use Negative Thinking

We need to learn to appreciate the power of negative thinking when it is applied in a constructive manner. We only should recognize negatives in order to avoid them.

For example, a tennis player does not need to be aware consciously of the net; a golfer, of the sand traps and water hazards; a bowler, of the channels; or a high jumper or pole-vaulter, of the bar. They all concentrate on their objectives or positive goals.

When this type of negative thinking is used, it operates to our advantage, not against us. It will always help us attain our various successes.

We need to take the following steps:

(1) We must be aware of the negative so that it can warn us of possible danger.

(2) We should evaluate the negative as being unwanted, objectionable, unacceptable and something that cannot result in happiness.

(3) We should then take whatever measures are necessary to correct the situation at once.

By employing this method and reacting in this manner, a form of *automatic reflex* is created. These correct reactions become part of our stored data. Thus we are using *negative feedback* as an automatic control which can actually guide us and help us remain clear of failure, thereby producing success.

Recognition of Negative Feedback

If we see *negative feedback* for what it is, a signal in the wrong direction, it will help to steer us toward the successful accomplishment of whatever we strive for. We need to be aware of our feelings about it, but must not concentrate on it. We also need to perceive it as objectionable and something we do not want to happen. It does not aid us in any way in producing happiness or success.

The inhibited individual is frustrated in almost every area of living when he cannot, to his own satisfaction, give voice to his thoughts and be himself. This feeling of unfulfillment will very likely extend into all of his activities.

Negative Feedback

In a feedback system, a negative signal is the same as disapproval, telling you that you're going in the wrong direction. It is necessary for you to take proper action that will guide you back in the right direction. The main concern of negative feedback is to alter and adjust the direction, not to halt it. Negative feedback is never a STOP sign. Its basic objective is to correct or change its forward direction and not to stop the action in its tracks.

Inhibitions caused by "What Others Think"

An inhibited personality is always aware of what other people think of him to the degree that he is too self-conscious about his actions. He is always weighing everything he says and does in an effort to please other people. Then he is too easily offended or his feelings become hurt by what someone thinks of him, or by what he *thinks* they think of him. Consequently, he acquires an inhibited personality and behaves in an unsatisfactory manner, merely because of excessive negative feedback.

To be effective with other people:
(1) Avoid trying too hard at the conscious level to impress them.
(2) Avoid doing or saying anything for the effect you believe it will have on them.
(3) Avoid thinking about what they think or feel about you.

Something to think about

Accentuate the positive, eliminate the negative (in terms of its influence on your actions).

22

Attitudes Can Be Changed

Our appoach is that attitudes can be changed How do we do this?—through a program of repetition.

Read the following each day for 7 days and it will impress on you the value of a daily, methodical systematic affirmation.

I am involved in a *daily, methodical, systematic* program toward direction of my chosen goals. By daily association with my positive attitudes, contained in my program, I will *think positive thoughts* —and *form the habit of thinking positively*. As this positive daily repetition builds up, it reflects itself in what I *do*. I will develop a conscious awareness of the difference between my *positive* and my *negative thoughts*.

Example:

(+ direction of your goal)

(− away from your goal)

I will concentrate on the positive and omit the negative in terms of its influence on my actions.

I will get positive action in the direction of my goals and this will start a constant upward spiral, stimulated by the very simple fact that my mind is like the *film* of *a camera* or the *tape of a recorder,* in that it absorbs everything it is exposed to. The net result is that, by exposure to my *daily systematic, methodical* program, I am involved in my *optimistic goal-oriented ideas.* My mind will then *associate and form habits* which will *show and express* themselves in my *ACTIONS.*

23

Plan Of Action

This Plan of Action is to be distinguished from the synthetic experiencing method (Data-Revision) in that it is in writing, and carries a deadline for its attainment of goals. Some of the thoughts and ideas generated by the synthetic method upon reaching the conscious level will be written down on the Plan of Action. Each of these methods will work separately, but they will work amazingly well if used together.

It is a well organized method of goal-setting. You already know that this is the "secret of success."

Goals are divided as follows:

Long-range Goals (tangible and intangible)
Must be meaningful . . . distant point of reference . . . something to aim at.

Short-range Goals (tangible and intangible)
Must be believable . . . steps toward long-range goals. Success by the yard is hard-by the inch is a cinch.

Motivational
Must be able to clearly see end results.
Must be compatible.

When goals are compatible you have a relaxed feeling every day that you are doing what you want to do. Your life will be what you desire to make it.

Some people have more opportunity, money and talent, but within certain limits do not have more time than anyone else. Therefore, *planning* is critical. Can you imagine the tremendous exhilaration that comes from having your life planned and doing what you want to do so that you don't waste time?

"People Don't Plan to Fail, They Fail to Plan"

Blueprint of finished product.

Plan in advance what you want your life to to be. Every day aim for what you are trying to accomplish. A written plan helps you visualize what it will mean to you if you continue this course. What do you do if you lose sight of the end result? The same is true in planning your life. Do you see how this would work for you? Do you see how this would make a tremendous difference in your performance?

> "ALL MEN SEEK *ONE GOAL: SUCCESS or HAPPINESS*. The only way to achieve TRUE SUCCESS is to express yourself completely in SERVICE to Society. *First, have a definite, clear, practical idea*-A GOAL, AN OBJECTIVE. *Second, seek the necessary MEANS TO ACHIEVE* your ends - wisdom, money, materials and methods. *THIRD, ADJUST ALL YOUR MEANS TO THAT END!"*
> —Aristotle

The plan of action is designed to put theory into *practice*, turn knowledge into *knowhow* and thought into *action*. It discourages procrastination and will move you to a greater utilization of your potential.

Your Own Plan of Action

A word of caution: *Do not* under any circumstances identify the plan of action as anything other than *yours*. Unless you make it your *own* plan it will remain forever outside your grasp and it will never make a significant change in your life. The "failure to identify" is critical. When you recognize the plan as *your plan* you will sense the power of your own talents, abilities and the capacity to *change*. Hereafter all references to this plan must be to *my plan of action*.

Crystalize your Thinking

The first step is to crystalize your thinking. It is a well known fact that only 5 percent of all people have definite, concrete plans for their achievement in life. Therefore it comes as no surprise that only 5 percent are highly successful.

With such clear-cut evidence of the *results* of planning, why are so many content with so little? Two reasons stand out prominently.

1. Very few people know how to plan.

2. Even fewer know how to *turn thought into action*. They have never really discovered the power of visualization. Thought is only the beginning of the process. Without "vivid imaging," without a crystal clear visualization of the "event" before we act, it never comes to pass. Everything we do we must first accomplish in our "imagination."

When you speak or think in vague generalities as "some day I'm going to have . . .," that day never comes. Before your energies can be directed toward your goal you must first *crystalize your thinking* and say exactly what you mean and exactly what you do want.

Set your *long-range goals* HIGH.

Set your *short-range goals*. (Progressive intermediate steps that are easy to reach.)

Visualize yourself as already being there.

133

Develop a Written Plan and
a Deadline for This Attainment.

The second step is to have a written plan and a deadline of its attainment, because *writing crystalizes thought* and *crystalized thought stimulates action.*

Definite plans produce definite results, but indefinite plans produce *no results.*

Unless a plan is committed to in writing, it is seldom definite.

1. The written plan will give you *direction,* now you will know:

Where you are now, and where you want to go.

A properly conceived plan in writing helps you in *both:* to see yourself in your present position clearly, exactly and honestly—and to define your objective just as accurately.

2. Planning conserves energy. You accomplish a great deal more with half the effort because your energies are *directed toward a goal.*

3. Planning assures compatibility. By reducing your goal to a written plan, uncompatible goals become more obvious.

4. Planning makes visualization habitual. The power of visualization has already been defined. No painting was ever painted that the artist could not clearly see in his imagination. Reducing a plan to writing makes visualization a habit—a habit that, once acquired, will open up a new world you never dreamed existed.

Each separate goal requires a deadline. A deadline gives a challenge to action. Without it, failure will follow, because your goal will be forgotten.

But deadlines carry hidden dangers unless you make them your slaves and not your master. What if you miscalculate and do not reach your goal by the deadline? What then? This is where most people accept temporary failure as defeat. If you have set the deadline you can change it.

The man who succeeds is the man who alters the *deadline,* but *not the goal*—who resets his sights in view of changing circumstances and keeps going until the goal is achieved (to be distinguished from Data-Revision in which no deadline is used).

Develop a Real Desire

The third step is to develop a real desire for the things you want from life.

Desire is based on a powerful emotion generated by crystalized thinking and vivid imagining.

Desire can be tested exactly and accurately by answering these seven questions:

1. What do I want? (Analyzed from previous procedure under goals.)
2. Where do I stand now?
3. What are the obstacles and road blocks? (What's between me and what I want?)
4. How can I overcome these obstacles? (Plan)
5. Target dates for overcoming obstacles?
6. What are the rewards?
7. IS IT REALLY WORTH IT TO ME?

When the answers to the questions are an integral part of your plan of action, you not only test your desire, but you can develop it and use it.

Develop Self-confidence

The fourth step is development of confidence in yourself and your ability. Confidence is a reliance on the positive (instead of the negative). Thoughts give direction to our conscious actions. All thoughts are basically positive. Only the direction is different.

A human being is limited by his self-imposed bonds of limitations. We can never come out from underneath these bonds *unless we believe we can change*—and we can change if we *think we can!* Everything tells us we can change; history speaks of progress and progress is *change;* biology speaks of evolution and evolution is change. Yet

135

some people stubbornly continue to believe that "others can change but I cannot."

People resist change for many reasons. Even when they decide to change, they try to change conscious actions before they change their self-image, their attitudes and their habits. Much of our activity is directed by the subconscious mind. Therefore any attempt to control the conscious is always ineffective.

Knowing *how* to change by changing our self-image, attitudes and habits, we build self-confidence in our ability. This self-confidence then becomes a way of life affecting everything we do.

Develop Determination

The last remaining ingredient is the development of *determination* to succeed regardless of circumstances or what "other people" say, think or do. In step three, if you have answered the question "is it worth it to me?" affirmatively and honestly, then you can find no circumstance that will allow you to sway from reaching your goal. You will develop your determination by:
1. Reviewing your written plan.
2. Concentrating on the rewards.

Your desire will stimulate an endless flow of dynamic, positive *direction* to keep you on course until your goals are reached.

Set goals and make plans for their achievement in the following areas of your life:

1. Spiritual
2. Mental
3. Physical
4. Social
5. Family Life
6. Financial

This kind of program will tell you *what to do* and *how to do it,* but *you* must do it. You link your thinking to a purpose. You know where you are going and your thoughts and actions are then concentrated on getting you there.

136

Long-range Goals	PROGRESS DATE Annual or Semiannual	Visual Aids
Tangible 1. 2. 3. **Intangible** 1. 2. 3.		

Short-range Goals	PROGRESS DATE Weekly or Monthly	Visual Aids
Tangible 1. 2. 3. **Intangible** 1. 2. 3.		

137

24

Tired People

Why Are There So Many Tired People?

Let's take the familiar problem as is so often expressed by doctors and psychologists whose patients declare, "Doctor, there must be something wrong with me. I seem to have so little energy." After a full examination the doctor reports there is nothing physically wrong. What do you suppose is the problem? Why do you think there are so many tired people? Once a person sees the tremendous amount of unnecessary and pointless burdens he is carrying around and disposes of them, he will no longer be tired. He must first become aware of these burdens. This is the problem of many, many people who are carrying around unnoticed loads of energy-robbing negative thoughts that steal their energy. No wonder they are all so tired.

Everyone has his special brand of energy-robbing burdens. The quicker we throw these away, the sooner we will feel better.

The feeling of being free is not a matter of gaining anything. It is purely a process of ridding ourselves of something. This is one of the most surprising, most rewarding and helpful ideas you can ever grasp.

The simplicity of this idea escapes most of us. We are all used to thinking in terms of joining, uniting and building, but our inner freedom lies in the opposite direction. *Happiness is a process of getting rid of these unnecessary burdens.* This is a vital truth. We must be able to clearly recognize the way to this truth doesn't lie in creating anything that does not now exist, or in acquiring anything not presently available. (It is all within our potential right now.)

25

Happiness

The Habit of Happiness

Dr. John A. Schindler (author of *How to Live 365 Days a Year*) explains happiness as, ". . . a state of mind in which our thinking is pleasant a good share of the time." This is a remarkable, deceptively simple definition. We don't think it could be stated more clearly.

Whole Physical System Works Better

When you are contented, you are usually in better health, are more efficient at your job and enjoy it more. Your brain works with greater competency and your memory is better when your mind is in a relaxed state. Your five senses are more acute when you think agreeable thoughts. Unhappiness and stress are causes of psychosomatic ailments.

It has been pointed out that when people in business have a positive bright outlook, they are more apt to succeed than those who are depressed.

Are You Being Manipulated?

When you react automatically to outside circumstances that tell you to be angry or to get upset, you are being manipulated into behavior which you might normally wish to avoid. You are letting outer conditions dictate how you act and feel. If you learn the *habit* of happiness, you are the master instead of the slave.

Happiness is a By-Product of a Goal

As we have said before, when a person is motivated toward a worthwhile, predetermined objective, he is usually a cheerful person. Conversely, when someone is happy, he will probably be successful. No one is really ever alive unless he is striving for a series of goals.

Happiness Can Be Methodically Cultivated

Anyone, by careful concentration, can develop the ability to keep his thoughts on a happy level a major portion of the time and methodically make cheerfulness a part of his behavior pattern.

On the surface, this may sound ridiculous and impossible. However, from our past observations, we have found that it is really unlikely anyone can make an optimistic outlook their way of life without earnest, intentional effort.

You may wait forever if you expect happiness to come to you as a matter of course or for someone to bring it to you. If you wait for your state of affairs to be perfect before you can have a pleasant frame of mind, you are destined to be gloomy, because that condition will probably never exist.

Nothing is ever all black or all white. Our lives are filled with gray days, and it is entirely our own decision as to which direction our thoughts will take. Whether or not we maintain optimistic thoughts is determined wholly by the type of thoughts we choose to keep in our minds.

Happiness

Happiness is the rarest, most prized, sought after state of man and, sadly, the least understood and most misunderstood.

We, as human beings, have a creative urge within us which gives us a deep desire to grow, solve problems and reach our goals. Accomplishing these things is the only way we can obtain peace of mind, fulfillment and happiness.

There can be no real happiness if the things we believe in are different from the things we do.

HAPPINESS is a by-product of a goal.

HAPPINESS is a mental attitude.

HAPPINESS is a state of mind in which our thinking is pleasant most of the time.

HAPPINESS is purely internal.

HAPPINESS is learned, and is practiced only in the present or never experienced at all.

HAPPINESS is a feeling of being glad, pleased, contented, doing well, peace, freedom, responding to life, being interested in life.

HAPPINESS is a mental habit.

HAPPINESS is an "emotional feeling" of satisfaction coming from having experienced or expecting something that, in your own opinion, is good or to your liking.

HAPPINESS is in your own personal terms, by your own standards, in your own way, in your own time, by yourself and for yourself. There is no comparative norm.

The achievement of a serene and lasting happiness is not an accident, nor is it a gift. It is something that each of us must construct for ourselves. We are not born happy. We learn to be happy.

Perpetual Happiness is Nonsense

It is pure absurdity to expect to be happy all the time. A periodic depression is normal. We all have enough common sense to know that anyone who is happy all the time may be in fact quite mad. After all, reality sometimes warrants unhappiness and you don't need to be apologetic or depressive about it. There's no need to feel that discontent is an occasion for immediate psychiatric suspicion. Perpetual happiness is nothing but nonsense. It is necessary to direct your attention to what is good, useful and productive and ignore all the rest.

Limitations on Thinking

We must literally limit the scope of our thinking. If we think of days gone by, we should create pictures in our minds of nostalgic occurrences, like happy, carefree events of our youth. When we think of the present, we must focus our minds on things that we strive to improve—our homes, our jobs and all our prospects for success. We must intentionally disregard situations that appear to have a dead end. When we think of the future, we should take for granted that all the things we want are a definite possibility.

Other Changes Come From the Inner

The most amazing effect of limiting our thinking is the dramatic change in the outer aspects of our lives which come about as a direct result of the inner transformation.

Self-image Consistent With Habits

Your habits are spontaneously altered when you change

143

your self-image, because these two things are closely allied. The self-image is compatible with your behavior pattern. Consequently, when you intentionally bring new patterns into being, you leave behind your old ones.

Happiness Does Not Lie in the Future, But In The Present

One of the problems shared most frequently by unhappy people is that they allow their lives to be governed by what may happen tomorrow. They are always waiting for some incident to come about in the future to make them happy —the time they get married, when the mortgage is paid off, when the children complete their education, when they make more money; when they get a new car, complete some job or overcome a difficulty. They are continually let down and frustrated.

If the art of being happy is not experienced and related to the present time, it will not be experienced at all. You cannot base happiness on an uncertain event or possible occurence. Another problem will always come along just as you find the answer to the previous one. Your whole life is a connecting succession of difficulties and problems—both large and small. The only time for happiness is right now.

Happiness Must Be Experienced

Happiness means being interested in life, or responding to life, not just with one's brain, but one's whole personality, and to become truly independent. Happiness can be negated by separating intellect and emotion. It requires a combination of experiencing, through intellect and feeling. Without this combination, man is incapable of experiencing anything but thought.

Being happy can be a decision between full human development and full marketplace success. It is tied into the capacity to see, to discern fact from fiction, not to indulge or live by rationalizations and illusions which block authentic experience. Care more for happiness than success.

The Only Cure is
The Curing of Unhappiness

A difficult person is an unhappy person. He is at war with himself and consequently is at war with the world. No happy person ever disturbed a meeting, preached a war, lynched a Negro, nagged a husband, wife, or children. No happy man ever committed a theft or murder. All crimes, hatred, all wars can be related to unhappiness. How does unhappiness arise and how does it ruin human lives?

Happiness is emotional tranquility. Unhappiness is emotional stress.

Learning Maturity Concept

Most people conduct their lives poorly because they have never been taught maturity. They have simply never learned to grow up mentally. Most of us continue to react to adult problems with childish reactions (conditioning). *It is by trying to meet adult problems with childish reactions that we generate emotional stress and/or unhappiness.* There is no place people are taught maturity. It does not come as a natural process. Maturity must be learned.

Maturity is a Matter of Attitudes

Maturity is not a matter of being crammed full of technical or classical knowledge or information, nor does it consist of being able to make important judgments correctly. It is essentially a collection of attitudes—attitudes that are more effective and helpful to the individual in meeting situations than are the attitudes of a small child in the same situation.

An attitude is an established way of reacting to certain classes of experience (Habit Pattern Conditioning). The more mature a person is, the more complete the stock of effective attitudes he can bring to the variety of experiences that arise in his day-to-day living. Areas which *require* the possession of maturity are Business, Sex, Old Age.

Is Financial Success
A Deterrent To Happiness

We believe there is a battle which every earnest human being has to fight with himself in order to make his life in accord with his beliefs. The instinct of acquisition hurries on from gain to gain, but the moral consciousness is very conservative. It has its roots deep in tradition of the past and therein comes each man's complications.

As soon as we get out into the world, there are only two possible courses open to us. Either we can try to make our lives conform to our beliefs, or we can modify our beliefs to fit our lives. True happiness, we know depends on which path we take.

Many men, in order to achieve financial success, force themselves to take the latter. They lose their idealism and become "practical" and indifferent toward "moral consciousness." Their material returns are high—but so is the price they pay. The moral consciousness eventually obtains its revenge—in ulcers, high blood pressure, alcoholism and in the kind of emotional collapse we wrongfully call "nervous breakdown."

The other task—that of shaping our lives to the pattern of our deepest beliefs—is infinitely more difficult and only a saint can perfectly succeed at all. But psychologically *it is the effort that counts,* not the achievement. When the moral consciousness is satisfied, a man can live comfortably with himself.

The unhappy man is constantly striving for the approval of others; yet the more applause he gets the more he re-

146

quires. The happy man is concerned only with his own approval, with knowledge that what he does is consistent with what he believes to be right.

Success is a blessing when it comes without compromising moral sense and the greatest of curses when it comes at the expense of silencing the inner voice.

26

Happiness Concept

Recognizing the Real Self
From The False Self

Inside every human is a "real" self and a "false" self. If the "real" part of your personality becomes a powerful force, you will undoubtedly become happier and more productive in all areas of your life. But if you permit the "false" self to take over control of your thoughts and behavior, you will probably become frustrated, with a feeling of emptiness and futility in your life.

In essence, *you* are the "real" self—positive, without negative qualities. It is really YOU, and you have always possessed it. The "false" self is negatively oriented, and even if it temporarily controls the "real" self, the real self is always there.

What does this have to do with personal happiness?

In order to be happy, a person must not permit the false self to dominate, because the false self remains miserable all the time. On the other hand, the real self, being positively oriented, is always happy.

When you are able to distinguish between your real and false selves, you will be taking a step to your goal of inner happiness. Your real self sends messages that tell you what to do, if you will merely listen.

Occasionally you may wonder why you should even try to develop new attitudes and forget your old negative ideas. What is the value and significance of understanding yourself and continuing to strive for self-improvement?

The value is uncomplicated and clear. Perhaps this is why many people do not understand it.

VALUE involves these facts:

THE POINT involves these facts:
You want to live the way you really want to.
You want control of your life.
You want to avoid mistakes.
You want an abundance of energy.
You want to always feel youthful.
You want to feel free of pressure.
You want to know who you are.
You want to look forward to a brighter tomorrow.
You want to feel free from fear.

These facts make up the VALUE, and they are available to everyone.

If you are aware that the complete value is to get the things you truly desire out of life and keep this in your mind, you will inevitably reach your goal.

Some people would like to get out of their rut and change their entire life style. However, they don't break away and live as they would like to because "they" have an artificial sense of morality.

"They" try to establish a false idea as to what your responsibilities are to them and what you owe them. The real fact is that "they" expect something from you. There is NOTHING you owe them. Remember that your primary obligation is to yourself.

Behaving in a manner that does no damage to you or to anyone else is genuine morality.

Think of your friendships and other relationships. It is a known fact that you are drawn to people who occupy the same level of consciousness that you do. When you change your self-image and thereby change your level of

149

awareness, you will have less in common with some of your friends and associates, including your shared psychological concerns. When you find associations at your new awareness level, they will probably be more rewarding.

Feeling obligated to help others is disturbing to some people.

You must learn not to confuse yourself with any notion as to how you can be of assistance to your fellow human beings. This idea is a terrible pitfall. Your wholehearted effort should be directed toward creating a new self-image. You should make this your primary obligation, the way in which you can be of service to others in the most beneficial way.

A person knows instinctively that you have within you firmness and power if he realizes you are trying to be someone to him and not necessarily trying to do something for him. Never try to do anything for anyone if it requires conscious effort; there is no need to help someone until it is automatic and you truly want to do so. You really don't want anything from someone you care for.

The way to be of the greatest service to someone else is by first changing your own self-image and developing your own inner strength. When you have accomplished this, you will never again be troubled about helping others. Your mental state will enable you to be someone to them, rather than to do something for them.

After this change has taken place and you have found your real self, you may be surprised at the extraordinary calmness and assurance you possess. Your relationships with other people will be more straightforward and open because you don't expect anything from each other. You can be close to one another and yet be independent at the same time.

Genuine kindness is what you are. It is not what you do. The greatest kindness you can ever offer anyone is the *truth*.

27
Exercises and Techniques

Begin each day a new and better way by reciting the following, and practicing each day for 21 days:

This is the beginning of a new day.

I have been given this day to use as I will.

What I do today is important,

because I'm exchanging a new day of my life for it.

When tomorrow comes, this day will be gone forever,

leaving in its place whatever I have traded for it.

I pledge to myself

that it shall be for gain, good, and success,

in order that I shall not regret the price I paid

for this day.

My thinking and my attitudes are calm and cheerful.

I act and feel friendly toward other people.

I am tolerant of other people, their shortcomings and mistakes, and I view their actions with the most favorable understanding possible.

I act as though attainment of my goals is certain to happen. I am the kind of individual I aspire to be, and everything I do and the way I feel expresses this individuality

I will not allow my judgment or attitude to be affected by negativism or pessimism.

I try to smile as often as possible, at least several times a day.

I respond in a calm and intelligent manner, without alarm, no matter what the situation.

If I cannot control a situation, I try always to react in a positive manner, even to negative facts.

Each of the above habitual ways of acting, feeling and thinking does have a beneficial and constructive influence on your self-image. Experience them daily and you will find a marked decrease in worry and sense of guilt and hostility and an increase in self-confidence.

Mark off 21 consecutive days after reciting each day.

1	2	3	4	5	6	7
8	9	10	11	12	13	14
15	16	17	18	19	20	21

It's Done With Mirrors

When you get what you want in your struggle for wealth
And the world makes you king for a day,
Just go to the mirror and look at yourself
And see what that man has to say.

For it isn't your father or mother or wife
Upon whose judgment you pass,
The fellow whose verdict counts most in your life
is the one staring back from the glass.

Some people may think you're a straight-shootin' chum
And call you a wonderful guy,
But the man in the glass says you're only a bum
If you can't look him straight in the eye.

He's the fellow to please, never mind all the rest
For he's with you clear to the end,
And you've passed your most dangerous, difficult test
If the man in the glass is your friend.

You may fool the whole world down the pathway of years

And get pats on the back as you pass,

But your final reward will be heartaches and tears

If you've cheated the man in the glass.

Practice this exercise by substituting first person pronouns (I, me, my).

Self Image Builders

We're not suggesting that you talk to the mirror. You must realize here that you are talking to the person in the mirror, and that person is the most important person in your life—YOU!

Self Image Builders

Your Mirror Magic Practice

Every morning, when you get up, do breathing exercises for a few minutes. Tell yourself you are taking in oxygen not only to satisfy your physical lungs but the lungs for your soul. Picture yourself not only stimulating the heart muscles of your body, but also the heart muscle of your mind and spirit. Tell yourself that you are making yourself strong enough to hurdle yesterday's fears and defeats to be strong for TODAY.

Go to the mirror every day for a few moments. Look at yourself. Ask yourself: "Am I a friend to myself?" . . . Remind yourself that you must be a friend to yourself before you can be a friend to others. Remind yourself again and again that you must rise above an error or a mistake of yesterday to be friendly to your self respect as a human being TODAY . . . Make a habit of it. . . .

> *"Do the thing and you will have the power."*
> Emerson

If you desire to improve yourself, remember this fact: Act the way you want to be (in your imagination), and you'll be the way you act.

Self Image Builders

Your Mirror Magic Practice

Are you the one in charge of wastebasket-emptying and garbage disposal in your home? If not, elect to be for at least six days. Utilize this usually onerous household task in a positive way as follows: As you throw away the garbage and useless accumulation of a busy household discard, at the same time, the emotional and mental garbage that you have allowed to accumulate in your mind. Thus, both your home and your self can start a new day clean and free.

Every day for six days when you leave your home and close the door, see this act as a symbolizing closing of the door to the past . . . That moment in the past when you made a mistake or failed in some undertaking, resolving that the past shall no longer intrude into your new day.

> *"Do the thing and you will have the power."*
> Emerson

If you desire to improve yourself, remember this fact: Act the way you want to be (in your imagination), and you'll be the way you act.

Self Image Builders

When you are driving your car or walking in the street and come to a red traffic light, every day for six days, think of the red light as an expression of your negative feelings, your fear of failure holding you back. Realize that no circumstance holds you back indefinitely. Expect the green light to go on opening the way for you to go ahead. Then when the green light flashes on, move forward as if you are moving toward a useful goal with the confidence of past successes, guiding you . . . giving you that winning feeling of accomplishment.

When God shuts one door—He opens another.

> *"Do the thing and you will have the power."*
> Emerson

If you desire to improve yourself, remember this fact: Act the way you want to be (in your imagination), and you'll be the way you act.

In Pursuit Of Success

The most useful rules are so deceptively simple as to escape recognition by most people. Heed the following very simple advice. These rules may not be easy to follow, but they are easy to understand.

1. *Do one thing at a time*
   Remember, no man can do more. Two or three things at a time are less than one thing at a time. Here mathematics stand confounded, for here always—more is less.

2. *Know the problem*
   Don't waste time trying to find answers to a problem when you don't know the problem. Be sure you have clearly stated the problem first.

3. *Learn to listen and listen to learn*
   Open your ears before you open your mouth—it may open your eyes.

4. *Learn to ask questions*
   The ability to ask questions made Socrates a wise man. Make it a point to ask questions if only to double check your position.

5. *Distinguish sense from nonsense . . . be brief!*
   Be not among those who expound brilliantly on "trivial matters." Be known for your succinct clarity and not for the "gift of gab."

6. *Accept change as inevitable*
Heraclitus said that "no man can step in the same river twice." Not only does the river change, but the man himself changes as well. Beware of the pat solution. Everything can be improved.

7. *Admit your mistakes*
Avoid the great temptation to rationalize your mistakes. Do not be afraid of making mistakes.

8. *Be simple*
If a child can understand, then so can an adult.

9. *Be calm*
Sound judgment is more likely to thrive in a contemplative atmosphere than in a hurricane.

10. *Smile*
A man with no humor can never have the warmth and personality of a great leader.

They Go Everywhere

A smile is quite a funny thing,
It wrinkles up your face.
And when it's gone you never find,
Its secret hiding place.

But far more wonderful it is,
To see what smiles can do.
He smiles at someone, since you smiled,
And so one smile makes two.

He smiles at someone, since you smiled,
And then that someone smiles back.
And that one smiles, until, in truth,
You fail in keeping track.

And since a smile can do great good,
By cheering hearts of care,
Let's smile and smile and not forget,
That smiles go everywhere! !

TAKE TIME TO

THINK	SEE YOURSELF AT YOUR BEST
PLAY	COUNT BLESSINGS
READ	USE CREATIVE IMAGINATION
LOVE	UNDERSTAND YOURSELF & OTHERS
PLAN	FEEL HAPPY
BE FRIENDLY	BE HAPPY (NOW)
LAUGH	FORGIVE YOURSELF & OTHERS
GIVE	BE CONSIDERATE
WORK	LEARN
RELAX	MAKE DECISIONS
BE HAPPY	BE CHEERFUL
FEEL FREE	DEVELOP HOBBIES
APOLOGIZE	SMILE
ADMIT ERROR	BE HAPPY
BEGIN OVER	BE RESPONSIVE (TO THE THINGS NEAR AT HAND)
SET GOALS	DEHYPNOTIZE FROM FALSE BELIEFS (REEVALUATE)
DREAM	

MY GREATEST MISTAKE IS TO:

be afraid to make a mistake.

live in the past.

worry about tomorrow.

compare myself (with others).

doubt myself.

not have confidence.

pass a negative judgment on myself and others.

not be happy NOW (not enjoy the present moment).

not improve my self-image.

not be a friend to myself.

not set goals.

not have a PMA (positive mental attitude).

not use my creative imagination.

not like my work.

get up tight and not relax.

not keep promises to myself.

not laugh at my mistakes.

not have a good hobby.

abuse my health.

inhibit my real personality.

say, "I can't, or I have to".

think I am not important.

not try to understand the other person's point of view.

not react calmly and intelligently.

give up.

ignore negative feedback.

be too concerned about what others think.

How To Make Decisions

Decisions

1. Get the facts.
2. Analyze and interpret the facts.
3. Arrive at a decison and then *act* on it.

> *"You have no right to an opinion*
> *until you have examined the evidence."*

If a man will devote his time to securing the facts in an impartial, objective way, his worries will evaporate in the light of knowledge. Merely writing the facts down and stating them clearly goes a long way toward a sensible solution.

> *"A problem well stated is half solved."*

1. What am I worried about?
2. What can I *do* about it?
3. *Decide* what to *do!*
4. *Start* immediately to *carry out* this decision.

Unless we *do* something about carrying out and actually *acting* on a decision, all our fact-finding and analyses are just whistling in the dark. Once a decision is made and acted on, dismiss all care and responsibility of its outcome. Don't reconsider, don't re-trace. It's the same as a roulette player having placed his bet and worrying about the outcome while the wheel is spinning, even though he has no longer any control.

> *"If you are going to worry, don't do it*
> *—If you do it—DON'T WORRY."*

166

Now Never Waits!

What happens to unused nows?
They turn into unusable thens.

JUST FOR TODAY
I will live through the next twelve hours and not tackle all my life's problems at once.

JUST FOR TODAY
in one thing I know I am equal with others—TIME. All of us draw the same salary in seconds, minutes and hours.

JUST FOR TODAY
I refuse to spend time worrying about what might happen. It usually doesn't. I am going to spend my time making things happen.

JUST FOR TODAY
I will stop saying, "If I had time . . ." I know I never will "find time" for anything. If I want time, I must make it.

JUST FOR TODAY
I will improve my mind. I will learn something useful. I will read something that requires effort, thought, and concentration.

JUST FOR TODAY
I will be agreeable. I will look my best, speak in a well modulated voice, and be courteous and considerate.

JUST FOR TODAY
I will not find fault with friends, relatives or colleagues. I will not try to change or improve anyone but myself.

JUST FOR TODAY
I will have a program. I will save myself from two enemies —hurry and indecision.

167

JUST FOR TODAY
I will exercise my character in three ways:
I will do a good turn and keep it a secret. (If anyone finds
out, it won't count.)
I will do two things I don't want to do, just for exercise.
I will be unafraid. Especially will I be unafraid to enjoy
what is beautiful, and believe that as I give to the world,
the world will give to me.

JUST FOR TODAY
I will have a quiet half hour all by myself, and relax. During this half hour, I will get a better perspective of my life.

JUST FOR TODAY
I will be happy.

Read every day for seven days.

What's The Problem?

Problems that complicate my life,
    That interrupt my plan,
Might be no task at all to solve,
    In the hands of another man.

Troubles I have, may not trouble him,
    and so it's plain to see,
If that problem's not there for the other one,
    The complication must be in me.

To Have A Friend

I'd like to have a friend sincere
   Loyal, considerate and kind.
Who's reliable, dependable,
   With a forgiving mind.

Unselfish, understanding,
   How patient he would be
It would be especially nice,
   If the friend I had was me.

H. Jay Halverson
A Psycho-Cybernetics Student

What I *have* today is a
direct result of what I *did*
yesterday; what I *will have*
tomorrow is a direct result
of what I *do* today. For
this reason it is useless
and silly for me to weep
over my present situation.

Yesterday is gone, and the
past cannot be changed.

If, however, I take action
now, I can form the future.

Work with what I have at the
moment and build upon it, is what I
must do, as it is in this way
only that I may have what I want.

—*Ray Gilbert*
A Student of Psycho-Cybernetics

A Reassuring Philosophy

When I was a young student I used to think that some-where out ahead lay a magic moment when I would be grown up and know all the answers. At that moment life would be easy: no more doubts, no uncertainties, and in each and every situation I would know exactly what to do.

Since then, many years have gone by, and one of the things I have really learned is that the moment of absolute certainty never comes. Along the way, while looking for the answers, I found that each of us looks at things differently, and that no one can ever be all right or know all the answers all the time.

I have come to the realization that the mark of an educated man is the ability to make a reasoned guess on the basis of what appears to be insufficient information. This observation implies simply that often, when a man is faced with decision, it is impossible for him to fill in all the uncertainties.

He cannot be sure he has every fact. And, so, in deciding, he must "guess." But this is precisely the point at which "education" comes in.

For, true education goes far beyond facts and classrooms. Education is experience and faith, courage and understanding and, most of all, the ability to think and act confidently.

These qualities will translate a dead knowledge into a living wisdom. They are what makes guesses turn out right.

—Arthur H. Schreiber

About the authors . . .

Maxwell Maltz, M.D. and Charles Schreiber have achieved national reputations as the foremost authorities on Psycho-Cybernetics.

Dr. Maltz is one of the first pioneers and fathers of plastic surgery in the United States. In New York from 1920 to early 1960, Dr. Maltz studied the changes which took place in his patients' personalities after he had corrected facial scars and disorders. Arising out of thousands and thousands of cases came his remarkable discovery of the "Self-Image," the most important psychologic discovery of this century. He is best known as the originator of the term "Psycho-Cybernetics" and as author of the best seller of the same name. His concepts were first printed in the book *Psycho-Cybernetics* in 1960, and since that time, over 15 million copies have been sold. This book is an important valuable contribution to man's knowledge of himself and his ability to improve himself. Most of his efforts since 1960 have been devoted to writing, traveling and lecturing world-wide on personal growth and understanding thru Psycho-Cybernetics.

Charles Schreiber had an active interest in the partnership of Charles and Arthur Schreiber Architects from 1938 until 1970. He has gained a national reputation as an architect, builder and planner, receiving 38 national awards since 1961. Among the Schreiber clients are the world renowned builders, Henry J. Kaiser and Del E. Webb. Mr. Schreiber attributes his personal success to the knowledge and application of the principles of Psycho-Cybernetics. Since early 1970 he has been actively associated with Dr. Maltz in presenting workshops on the application of Psycho-Cybernetic principles in Arizona and the rest of the nation. Dr. Maltz recognized Mr. Schreiber as the foremost practitioner of Psycho-Cybernetics, and appointed him National Director of Workshops in 1973.

Recommended Readings

- Riches Are Your Right by Joseph Murphy

- The Money Illusion by Irving Fisher

- How To Win Friends And Influence People: A Condensation From The Book by Dale Carnegie

- How to Make a Fortune Today-Starting from Scratch: Nickerson's New Real Estate Guide by William Nickerson

- How I Trade and Invest in Stocks and Bonds by Richard D. Wyckoff

- The Magic of Believing by Claude M. Bristol

- Scientific Advertising by Claude C. Hopkins

- The Law of Success: Using the Power of Spirit to Create Health, Prosperity, and Happiness by Paramahansa Yogananda

- How I Learned the Secrets of Success in Selling by Frank Bettger

- The W. D. Gann Master Commodity Course: Original Commodity Market Trading Course by W. D. Gann

Available at www.snowballpublishing.com

Lightning Source UK Ltd.
Milton Keynes UK
UKHW011219170620
365157UK00002B/222